THE CHRONICLE

OF

JOSHUA THE STYLITE.

THE CHRONICLE

OF

JOSHUA THE STYLITE,

COMPOSED IN SYRIAC

A.D. 507,

WITH A TRANSLATION INTO ENGLISH

AND NOTES

BY

W. WRIGHT, LL.D.,

PROFESSOR OF ARABIC IN THE UNIVERSITY OF CAMBRIDGE.

EDITED FOR THE SYNDICS OF THE UNIVERSITY PRESS.

CAMBRIDGE:

AT THE UNIVERSITY PRESS.

1882

CAMBRIDGE UNIVERSITY PRESS
Cambridge, New York, Melbourne, Madrid, Cape Town,
Singapore, São Paulo, Delhi, Mexico City

Cambridge University Press
The Edinburgh Building, Cambridge CB2 8RU, UK

Published in the United States of America by Cambridge University Press, New York

www.cambridge.org
Information on this title: www.cambridge.org/9781107621053

First published 1882
First paperback edition 2013

A catalogue record for this publication is available from the British Library

ISBN 978-1-107-62105-3 Paperback

PREFACE.

I. THE Chronicle of Joshua (ܝܶܫܽܘܥ, Yêshûaʿ or Jesus) the Stylite has been long known to historians in the abridged Latin translation of Joseph Simon Assemâni (السَّمْعاني), which occupies pp. 262—283 of the first volume of his *Bibliotheca Orientalis*; and it is generally acknowledged to be one of the most valuable authorities for the period with which it deals[*]. The first complete edition of the Syriac text did not, however, appear till 1876, when it was edited for the German Oriental Society, with a French translation and many useful notes[†], by the well known orientalist the Abbé P. Martin, to whose industry scholars are indebted for various important Syriac publications.

That this *editio princeps* should be faulty in many respects was unavoidable, partly from the fact that the editor had only a single not very clearly written manuscript for the basis of his text, and partly because circumstances prevented him from re-collating his copy with the original before putting it to press. It was reviewed by Professor Noeldeke of Strassburg in the *Zeitschrift der Deutschen Morgenländischen Gesellschaft*, Bd xxx, pp. 351—8, where he proposed many excellent emendations. Having read the book through several times with pupils, I sent

---

[*] See, for example, the numerous references to it in Lebeau, *Histoire du Bas-Empire*, ed. Saint-Martin, t. vii, especially in book xxxviii.

[†] See *Abhandlungen für die Kunde des Morgenlandes herausgegeben von der Deutschen Morgenländischen Gesellschaft. VI. Band. No. I. Chronique de Josué le Stylite écrite vers l'an 515, texte et traduction par M. l'abbé Paulin Martin.*

to Professor Noeldeke a further list of corrections, shortly before
the publication of his Syriac Grammar in 1880, and we
exchanged several letters on the subject. Since then another
friend, Professor Ignazio Guidi of Rome, has most kindly supplied me with a fresh collation of the entire work; and I am
thus enabled to lay a tolerably correct text before the reader,
without having much recourse to conjectural emendation. If I
have not described certain readings of my text as corrections
made by this or that scholar, it is because I have ascertained,
thanks to Guidi's unwearying kindness, that they are the actual
readings of the original manuscript. Thus I could not credit
M. Martin himself with ܟܣܝܘܐܠ (p. 18, l. 15), and with ܟܪܝܚܣܡܠ
(p. 88, l. 2); nor Professor Noeldeke with ܟܠܣܟ ܕܗܣ ܒ ܐܠܠܗ
(p. 48, l. 6), and with ܩܘܟܘܥ ܘܟܥܠ ܗ ܕ ܘܟ ܟܥܕܟ ܙܟܠܟ ܗܘܘ (p. 85,
l. 1); nor Mr Bensly, of Gonville and Caius College, with ܩܣܣ
(p. 3, l. 13); nor my former pupil Mr Keith-Falconer with
ܟܠܣܟܣ (p. 49, l. 5); nor myself with ܟܕ (p. 29, l. 13), and
with ܐܟܪܘ (p. 34, l. 8). I have never altered the actual readings
of the manuscript, so far as I am aware, without giving due
warning thereof in the notes. I have, however, taken the
liberty, with the view of facilitating the task of the reader,
of adding a considerable number of diacritical points, especially
in the verbal forms. From the interpunction of the manuscript,
on the other hand, I have but rarely deviated, and then only
when it seemed to me to be absolutely necessary.

In my translation I have striven to be as literal as the difference between the two idioms will allow. My method is first
to translate as closely as I can, and then to try if I can improve
the form of expression in any way without the sacrifice of truthfulness to the original. I also endeavour to preserve a somewhat
antiquated and Biblical style, as being peculiarly adapted
to the rendering into English of Oriental works, whether
poetical or historical. The Old Testament and the Kor'ân,

which are, of course, in many ways strikingly similar in their diction, can both be easily made ridiculous by turning them into our modern vernacular, particularly if we vulgarize with malice prepense.

In my version I have sometimes expressed the sense of a conjectural emendation rather than of the manuscript reading. The comparison of the Syriac text and the critical notes will readily show the attentive reader when this is the case. Words which I have found it necessary to add for the sake of the English form of expression, or of greater clearness, I have commonly put within parentheses ( ); but where an actual lacuna in the text is supplied by conjecture, I have employed brackets [ ].

Of the notes I think it necessary to say no more than that they are intended chiefly for non-orientalists and for those who are beginning their oriental studies. It seemed to me to be quite superfluous to repeat the historical information contained in the copious annotations of Assemâni and of the Abbé Martin. In matters relating to the topography of Edessa and its district I have had recourse to my friend Professor G. Hoffmann of Kiel, who is probably the best acquainted of living orientalists with the geography of Mesopotamia and the adjacent countries. A comprehensive work on the subject from his hand would be a boon to all scholars. The plan of Edessa is taken from Carsten Niebuhr's *Voyage en Arabie, et en d'autres Pays circonvoisins, traduit de l'Allemand,* 1780, t. ii, p. 330, with additions and alterations suggested by Professor Hoffmann. As for the rough map of the seat of war, it is only reproduced from an ordinary atlas.

I have endeavoured, for the convenience of readers, to conform my edition in externals, as far as possible, to that of the Abbé Martin; and I would therefore have gladly adopted his numeration of the chapters, but found it to be impossible. In the first place, I had to strike out his seventh chapter, which

is merely the final note of a scribe of much later date. This
reduces the number of chapters by one from VIII (now VII) to
XCI (now XC). But, in the second place, I had to unite his
chapters XCI and XCII, the lacuna on p. 75 of his edition being
imaginary. Consequently the number of chapters from here to
the end is reduced by two, and Martin's ch. XCIII is in my
edition XCI.

II. We owe the preservation of the short Chronicle of
Joshua the Stylite to the care of a later historian, Dionysius of
Tell-Maḥrê*, patriarch of the Jacobites (ob. A. Gr. 1156, A.D.
845)†, who incorporated it with his own larger work, which
deserves to be made accessible to students of history without
further delay‡. The solitary manuscript of this work which has
come down to our times is preserved in the Vatican Library§.
It is in great part palimpsest, the underlying text being Coptic.
According to Assemâni, *Bibl. Orient.*, t. ii, pp. 98, 99, it was
written in the Nitrian desert when Moses of Nisîbis was abbot
of the convent of S. Mary Deipara, that is to say, between
A.D. 907 and 944 (see my *Catalogue of Syriac MSS. in the
British Museum, General Index*, p. 1310); but in his *Catal. Codd.
Manuscriptorum Biblioth. Apostol. Vaticanae*, t. iii, p. 328, no.
CLXII, he asserts that it was one of those volumes which Moses
of Nisîbis brought back with him to the Nitrian Convent in 932,
after his visit to Baghdâd and his journey through Mesopotamia ‖.

* ﻟﻜﺴﻤﺘﺍ, in Arabic ﺗﻞ ﻣﻜﺮﻱ, a small town on the river Balîkh,
between ar-Raḳḳah and Ḥiṣn Maslamah, according to Yâḳût in the *Mu'jam
al-Buldân.*

† See Assemâni, *Bibl. Orient.*, t. ii, p. 98 sqq., and pp. 344—8.

‡ The Swedish orientalist Professor Tullberg of Upsala began an edition of it
in 1850, which will, I hope, be completed by Professor Ign. Guidi.

§ Dionysius has placed the Chronicle of Joshua immediately after the
Henôtikon of Zênôn, without any prefatory remarks.

‖ If so, the note to that effect has disappeared from the manuscript. It must
be remarked, however, that the volume is much damaged, and that some of the
worst pages have been covered at a recent period with "carta vegetale". The
result is that the writing is no longer legible or barely so.

Of Joshua we know little more than what he has himself thought fit to tell us. He wrote his Chronicle at the request of one Sergius, the abbot of a convent in the district of Edessa (ch. I), to whom he repeatedly addresses himself in the course of it. The last date which occurs in it is 28th November A.D. 506 (ch. C); and considering the tone of the final chapter, I have thought myself justified in assigning the composition of the work to that winter and the earlier part of the following year, which is also Noeldeke's opinion (*Zeitschrift d. D. M. G.*, Bd xxx, p. 352)*. A more recent copyist, who supplied a lacuna in the manuscript of Dionysius†, adds some details regarding Joshua as follows (see Martin's edition, p. 8).

ܨܠܘ ܥܠ ܐܠܝܫܥ ܕܘܝܐ ܡܢ ܥܘܡܪܐ ܕܙܘܩܢܝܢ ܕܟܬܒ ܦܬܩܐ
ܗܢܐ ܕܢܫܟܚ ܐܝܟ ܓܝܣܐ ܕܡܢ ܝܡܝܢܐ܆ ܐܡܝܢ ܘܐܡܝܢ. ܀
ܢܗܘܘܢ ܬܫܒܘܚܬܗ ܕܐܠܗܐ ܒܪܐ ܦܪܘܩܢ ܝܫܘܥ ܡܫܝܚܐ ܥܠ
ܩܕܝܫܐ ܡܪܝ ܝܫܘܥ ܐܣܛܘܠܝܛܐ ܡܢ ܕܝܪܐ ܕܙܘܩܢܝܢ. ܕܟܬܒ
ܟܬܒܐ ܗܢܐ ܕܥܘܗܕܢܐ ܗܢܐ (delete this word?) ܕܐܘܠܨܢܐ ܕܒ̈ܝܫܬܐ‡
ܕܗܘܘ ܒܐܘܪܗܝ ܘܐܡܕ ܘܒܟܠܗ ܗܘ̇ ܛܘܪܐ ܒܝܬ ܢܗܪ̈ܝܢ ܀

"Pray for the wretched Elisha, from the convent of Zûḳnîn (near Âmid), who wrote this leaf, that he may find grace like the thief on the right hand. Amen and Amen. May the

* The first sentence of the last chapter is no doubt an addition by a later writer, perhaps Dionysius of Tell-Maḥrê himself.

† The preface from p. 1 to p. 6, l. 10, ܓܢܣܐ ܗܘ, is in the same hand as the bulk of the manuscript. From that point to p. 8, l. 11, is in the handwriting of Elisha of Zûḳnîn. The next leaf of the manuscript begins with the words, p. 8, l. 10, ܕܡܬܦܓܓܝܢ ܐܝܟ ܡܐ ܕܡܫܒܚ ܐܢܬ ܠܡܫܬܡܠܝܘ ܡܢ ܗܢܝܢ ܕܟܬܒ ܐܢܐ ܠܟ ܀ ܕܡܫܡܫܢܐ ܫܡܥܬ ܩ̈ܛܠܐ ܘܠܒܫ ܘܡ. There is also a modern copy of the preface and introduction, on European paper, as far as p. 11, l. 14, ܘܡܛܠ ܕܢܗܘܐ ܠܡܐܢܐ ܕܡܗܝ̈ܡܢܐ ܕܠܒܘܬܗ.

‡ Not ܕܐܘܠܨܢܐ ܒ̈ܝܫܬܐ, as Assemâni has given in the *Bibl. Orient.*, t. i. p. 260, col. 2.

mercy of the great God and our Redeemer Jesus Christ be upon
the priest Mâr Yêshûa' (Joshua) the stylite, from the convent of
Zûḳnîn, who wrote this Chronicle of the evil times that are past,
and of the calamities and troubles which the (Persian) tyrant
wrought among men."

W. WRIGHT.

QUEENS' COLLEGE, CAMBRIDGE.
23 *April*, 1882.

CORRIGENDA.

In the Syriac text: Page 2, l. 3, read ⟨Syriac⟩.—Page 19, l. 9, perhaps
we might read ⟨Syriac⟩ instead of ⟨Syriac⟩; "he used every day to thrust
himself into his presence, and importunately ask him to give him" *etc.*—Page
25, l. 18, read ⟨Syriac⟩.—Page 36, l. 12, read ⟨Syriac⟩.—Page 46, l. 13, read
⟨Syriac⟩.—Page 57, l. 22, add ⟨Syriac⟩ after ⟨Syriac⟩?—Page 61, l. 11, read
⟨Syriac⟩.

In the English translation: Page 65, last line, Read: "at Âmid. With the
view.........of peace, he also sent" *etc.*

A HISTORY OF THE TIME OF AFFLICTION AT ÔRHÂI* AND ÂMID† AND THROUGHOUT ALL MESOPOTAMIA.

I. I have received the letter of thy Godloving holiness, O most excellent of men, Sergius, priest and abbot, in which thou hast bidden me write for thee, by way of record, (concerning the time) when the locusts came, and when the sun was darkened, and when there was earthquake and famine and pestilence, and (about) the war between the Greeks‡ and the Persians§. But

---

* ܐܘܪܗܝ Ôrhâi or Ûrhâi, الرُّها ar-Ruhâ, called by the Greeks Ἔδεσσα, now Orfah or Urfah. I have elsewhere used the Greek name.

† أَمِدْ, Ἄμιδα, ܐܡܝܕ, now called Ḳara Âmid (Black Âmid) or Diyâr-bekr (دِيَار بَكَر).

‡ ܪ̈ܗܘܡܝܐ or ܪ̈ܘܡܝܐ, literally, the Romans; but Constantinople was nova Roma, 'Ρώμη νέα, and hence the Syrians and Arabs use the words ܪ̈ܘܡܝܐ and الرُّوم, ar-Rûm, to designate the Byzantine Greeks.

§ ܦܲܪ̈ܣܳܝܐ, Pârsâyê, elsewhere written ܦܘܪ̈ܣܝܐ, Pârsâyê or Pûrsôyê. It has been thought that the spelling ܦܘܪ̈ܣܝܐ is meant to be insulting, as if connecting the word with ܦܘܪ̈ܣܝܐ, exposure, shame, disgrace, τὰ αἰδοῖα. I can hardly imagine this to be correct (see Cureton, Spicil., p. 14, ll. 16—19; Wright, Catalogue, p. 1161, col. 2, ll. 4, 20; and compare in the present work, in ch. xc, ܦܘ̈ܩܕܐ for ܦܘ̈ܩܕܐ). To me it appears that it is only an example of the gradually weakening vowel-series â, å, ô, û; as in ܩܘ̈ܡܐ, ܩܘ̈ܡܬܐ; ܚ̈ܟܝܢܐ, ܚ̈ܟܝܢܘܬܐ, etc.; not to mention Persian and Teutonic analogies.

besides these things, there were found therein great encomiums of myself, which made me much ashamed even when alone with my own soul, because not one of them pertains to me in reality. Now I would fain write the things that are in thee, but the eye of my understanding is unable to examine and see, such as it actually is, the marvellous robe (στολή) which thy energetic will hath woven for thee and clothed thee therewith; for it is clearly manifest that thou burnest with the love that fulfils the law, since thou carest not only for the brethren that are under thy authority at this time, but also for all the lovers of learning that may hereafter enter thy blessed monastery; and in thy diligence thou wishest to leave in writing memorials of the chastisements which have been wrought in our times because of our sins, so that, when they read and see the things that have befallen us, they may take warning by our sins and be delivered from our punishments. One must wonder at the fulness of thy love, which is poured out upon all men, that it is not exhausted nor faileth. Indeed I am unable to speak of it as it is, because I have not been nigh unto its working; nor do I know how to tell about it from a single interview which I have had with thee.

II. Like Jonathan, the true friend, thou hast bound thyself to me in love. But that the soul of Jonathan clave unto the soul of David, after he saw that the giant was slain by his hands and the camp delivered, is not so marvellous as this, because he loved him for his good deeds; whereas thou hast loved me more than thyself, without having seen anything that was good in me. Nor is Jonathan's delivering of David from death at the hands of Saul deserving of wonder in comparison with this (doing) of thine, because he still requited unto him something that was due to him; for he first delivered him from death, and gave life unto him and all his father's house, that they should not die by the hands of the Philistine. And though nothing like this has been done by me unto thee, thou art at all times praying unto God for me, that I may be delivered from Satan, and that he may not slay me through sins. But this I must say, that thou lovest me as David did Saul; for thou art intoxicated by the greatness of thy affection to such a degree that, because of the fervency of thy love, thou knowest not what my measure is, but imaginest regarding me things which are far beyond me. For in the time preceding this, thou didst supply my deficiencies by the teaching contained in thy letters; and thou didst take such care for me as parents do, who, though they have not profited aught by their children, yet care for everything that they need. And today in thy discretion thou hast humbled thyself, and hast begged me to write for thee things that are too hard for me, that hereby thou mightest be especially exalted; and though thou knowest them better than I do, thou wishest to learn them from me. So neither do I grudge thee this, nor do I decline to do what thou hast commanded.

III. Know then that I too, when I saw these signs that were wrought and the chastisements that came after them, was thinking that they were worthy of being written down and preserved in some record, and not let fall into oblivion. But whereas I considered the weakness of my mind and my own utter ignorance (ἰδιωτεία), I declined to do this. Now however that thou hast bidden me do this very thing, I am in such fear as a man who, not knowing how to swim well, is ordered to go down into deep waters. But because I rely on thy prayers to draw me out, which are constantly sent up by thee unto God on my behalf, I believe that I shall be providentially saved from drowning and drawn forth from the sea into which thou hast cast me; since I shall swim as best I can in its shallows, because its depths cannot be explored. For who is able to tell fittingly concerning those things which God hath wrought in His wisdom to wipe out sins and to chastise offences? For the exact nature of God's government is hidden even from the angels, as thou mayest learn from the parable of the tares in the Gospel*. For when his servants said unto the master of the house, "Wilt thou that we go and gather them up?" he that knew the things as they were said unto them, "Nay, lest while ye gather up the tares, ye root up also the wheat with them." This then we say according to our knowledge, that because of the multitude of our sins our chastisements were abundant; and had not the protection of God embraced the whole world so that it should not be dissolved, the lives of all mankind would probably have perished. For at

* S. Matthew, ch. xiii. 24.

what times did afflictions like these happen with such violence, save in these (times) in which we live? And because the cause of them has not been removed, they have not even yet ceased. In addition to that which we saw with our own eyes and heard with our own ears, and amid which we lived, there terrified us also rumours from far and near, and calamities that befel in various places; terrible earthquakes, overturnings of cities, famines and pestilences, wars and tumults, captivity and deportation of whole districts, rasings and burning of churches. And whereas these things have amazed thee by their frequency, thou hast sent unto me to write them down with words of grief and sorrow, which shall astonish both readers and hearers; and I know that thou hast said this through thy zeal for good things, that there may be contrition also in those who hear them, and that they may draw nigh unto repentance.

IV. But know that it is one thing for a man to write sadly, and another (to write) truly; for any man who is endowed with natural eloquence can, if he chooses, write sad and melancholy tales. But I am a plain man in speech, and I record in this book those things which all men that are in our country can testify to be true; and it is for them who read and hear, when they have examined them, if they please, to draw nigh unto repentance. But perchance one may say, "What profit have those who read from these things, if admonition be not mingled with the recital?" I for my part, as one who is not able to do this, say that these chastisements which have come upon us are sufficient to rebuke us and our posterity, and to teach us by the memory and reading of them that they were sent upon us for our sins. If they did not teach us this, they would be quite useless to us. But this cannot be said, because chastisements supply to us the place of teaching; and that they are sent upon us for our sins all believers under heaven testify, in accordance with the words of S. Paul, who says *, "When we are chastened, we are chastened of the Lord, that we should not be condemned with the world." For the whole object of men being chastened in this world is that they may be restrained from their sins, and that the judgement of the world to come may be made light for

* 1 Corinthians, ch. xi. 32.

them. As for those who are chastised because of sinners, whilst they themselves have not sinned, a double reward shall be added unto them. But there is mercy at all times even for those who are unworthy, because of the kindness and grace and longsuffering of God, who willeth that this world should last until the time that is decreed in His knowledge that forgetteth not. And that these things are so is clear both from the evidences of holy Scripture and from the things that have taken place among us, which we purpose to write down.

V. For behold, there leaned heavily upon us the calamities of hunger and of pestilence in the time of the locusts, so that we were well nigh going to destruction; but God had mercy upon us, though we were unworthy, and gave us a little respite * from the calamities that pressed upon us. And this, as I have said, was because of His goodness. But He changed our torments, after we had had some respite, and smote us by the hands of the Assyrian, who is called the rod of anger †. Now I do not wish to deny the free will of the Persians, when I say that God smote us by their hands ; nor do I, after God, bring forward any blame of their wickedness; but reflecting that, because of our sins, He has not inflicted any punishment on them, I have set it down that He smote us by their hands. Now the pleasure of this wicked people is abundantly made evident by this, that they have not shown mercy unto those who were delivered up unto them ; for they have been accustomed to show their pleasure and to rejoice in evil done to the children of men, wherewith the Prophet too taunts them and says, prophesying regarding the desolation of Babylon as it were by the mouth of the Lord‡: "I was wroth with my people, who defiled mine inheritance ; and I delivered them into thy hands, and thou didst show them no mercy." Unto us too, therefore, they have similarly wrought harm in their pitiless pleasure, according to their wont. For though the rod of their chastisement did not reach our bodies, and they were unable to make themselves masters of our city, (because it is not possible for the promise of Christ to be made void, who promised the believing king Abgâr, saying, "Thy city shall be blessed, and no enemy

---

* ܩܝܣܐ, ܩܐܠܐ, "breathing-space."   † Isaiah, ch. x. 5.

‡ Isaiah, ch. xlvii. 6.

shall ever make himself master of it*";) yet, because of the believers who were spoiled and led away captive and slain and destroyed in the other cities which were captured, and who were like mud in the streets, all those have tasted no small degree of suffering who have learned to sympathise with them that suffer. And those too who were far away from this (sight) have been tortured with fear for their own lives by their lack of faith, for they thought that the enemy would make himself master of Edessa too, as he had done of other cities. About which things we are going to write unto thee.

VI. Since then, according to the saying of the wise Solomon†, "War is brought about by provocation"; and thou wishest to learn this very thing, namely by what causes it was provoked; it is my intention to inform thee whence these causes took their rise ‡, even at the risk of its being thought that I speak of things the time of which is long past. And then, after a little, I will make known to thee too how these causes acquired strength. For although this war was stirred up against us because of our sins, yet it took its origin in certain obvious facts, which I am going to relate to thee, that thou mayest be clearly acquainted with the whole subject, and not be led, along with some foolish persons, to blame the all-ruling and believing emperor Anastasius. For he was not the exciting cause of the war, but it was provoked from a much earlier time, as thou mayest understand from the things that I am going to write unto thee.

VII. In the year 609 (A.D. 297—8)§ the Greeks got possession of ‖ the city of Nisîbis ¶, and it remained under their

---

* On the promise of our Lord to king Abgâr that Edessa should never be captured by an enemy, see Cureton, *Ancient Syriac Documents*, p. 10 and p. 152; Phillips, *The Doctrine of Addai*, p. ܐ and p. 5; Lipsius, *Die Edessenische Abgar-Sage kritisch untersucht* (Braunschweig, 1880), pp. 16—21.

† Proverbs, ch. xxiv. 6.   ‡ Literally, *called*.

§ The era of Alexander, or of the Greeks, begins with October 312 B.C.

‖ The MS. has *built* or *rebuilt*, ܐܒܢܐ ; but we should probably read either *sacked*, ܒܙܐ, or *got possession of*, ܐܚܕ. The former has the support of a similar passage in chapter xlviii.

¶ Νάσιβις, Νέσιβις or Νίσιβις, Nisîbis. نَصِيبِين Naṣîbîn.

sway for sixty-five years. After the death of Julian in Persia, which took place in the year 674 (A.D. 362—3), Jovinian*, who reigned over the Greeks after him, preferred peace above everything; and for the sake of this he allowed the Persians to take possession of Nisîbis for one hundred and twenty years, after which they were to restore it to its (former) masters. These years came to an end in the time of the Greek emperor Zênôn; but the Persians were unwilling to restore the city, and this thing stirred up strife.

VIII. Further, there was a treaty between the Greeks and the Persians, that, if they had need of one another when carrying on war with any nation, they should help one another, by giving three hundred able-bodied men, with their arms and horses, or three hundred staters (estîrâ, στατήρ) in lieu of each man, according to the wish of the party that had need. Now the Greeks, by the help of God, the Lord of all, had never any need of assistance from the Persians; for believing emperors have always reigned from that time until the present day, and by the help of Heaven their power has been strengthened. But the kings of the Persians have been sending ambassadors and receiving money for their needs; but it was not in the way of tribute that they took it, as many thought.

IX. Even in our days Pêrôz†, the king of the Persians, because of the wars that he had with the Kûshânâyê or Huns‡, very often received money from the Greeks, not however demanding it as tribute, but exciting their religious zeal, as if he was carrying on his contests on their behalf, "that," said he, "they may not pass over into your territory." What made these words of his find credence was the devastation and depopulation § which the Huns wrought in the Greek territory

---

* That is, Jovian. See Noeldeke in the *Zeitschrift der Deutschen Morgenländischen Gesellschaft*, Bd xxviii, p. 263, note 2.

† See Noeldeke, *Geschichte der Perser und Araber zur Zeit der Sasaniden*, translated from aṭ-Ṭabarî, p. 117, with note 2.

‡ See the references to Noeldeke's *Geschichte der Perser* u. s. w., in the note on the Syriac text.

§ ܫܒܐ, the carrying away captive of the inhabitants into slavery. ܓܠܘܬܐ is the deportation of the whole population from one district to another. See ch. iii.

in the year 707 (A.D. 395—6), in the days of the emperors
Honorius and Arcadius, the sons of Theodosius the Great, when
all Syria was delivered into their hands by the treachery of the
prefect* Rufinus and the supineness of the general (στρατηλάτης)
Addai.

X.   By the help of the money which he received from the
Greeks, Pêrôz subdued the Huns, and took many places from
their land and added them to his own kingdom; but at last he
was taken prisoner by them.   When Zênôn, the emperor of the
Greeks, heard this, he sent money of his own and freed him,
and reconciled him with them.   Pêrôz made a treaty with the
Huns that he would not again cross the boundary of their
territory to make war with them; but he went back from and
broke his covenant, like Zedekiah†, and went to war, and like
him he was delivered into the hands of his enemies, and all his
army was destroyed and dispersed, and he himself was taken
alive.   He promised in his pride that he would give for the
safety of his life thirty mules laden with silver coin‡; and he
sent to his country over which he ruled, but he could hardly
collect twenty loads, for by his former wars he had completely
emptied the treasury of the king who preceded him.   Instead
therefore of the other ten loads, he placed with them as a
pledge and hostage (ὅμηρος) his son Ḳawâd §, until he should
send them, and he made an agreement with them for the
second time that he would not again go to war.

XI.   When he returned to his kingdom, he imposed a poll-
tax ‖ on his whole country, and sent the ten loads of silver coin,
and delivered his son.   But he again collected an army and
went to war; and the word of the Prophet was in very reality
fulfilled regarding him, who says ¶, "I saw the wicked uplifted
like the trees of the forest, but when I passed by he was not,
and I sought him but did not find him."   For when a battle

---

* Ὕπαρχος τοῦ πραιτωρίου or τῆς αὐλῆς.   See Du Cange, *Glossarium ad
Scriptores mediae et infimae Graecitatis*, Ἔπαρχος.

† 1 Kings, ch. xxiv. 20; 2 Chronicles, ch. xxxvi. 13; Jeremiah, ch. lii. 3.

‡ ܙܘܙܐ, *zûzê*, drachmas or dirhams.

§ See Noeldeke, *Gesch. d. Perser* u. s. w., p. 135, note 1.

‖ ܟܣܦ ܪܫܐ, *head-money*.

¶ Psalm xxxvii, 35, 36.

took place, and the two hosts* were mingled together in confusion, his whole force was destroyed, and he himself was sought but not found; nor to the present day is it known what became of him, whether he was buried under the bodies of the slain, or threw himself into the sea, or hid himself in a cave under ground and perished of hunger, or concealed himself in a wood and was devoured by wild beasts.

XII. In the days of Pêrôz the Greek empire too was in disorder; for the officials of the palace (παλάτιον) hated the emperor Zênôn because he was an Isaurian by race, and Basiliscus† rebelled against him and became emperor in his stead. Afterwards, however, Zênôn strengthened himself and was reestablished on the throne. And because he had had experience of the hatred of many towards him, he prepared for himself an impregnable fortress‡ in his own country; so that, if any harm should befal him, it might be a place of refuge for him. His confidant in this was the military governor (στρατη-λάτης) of Antioch, by name Illus, who was likewise an Isaurian; for he bestowed posts of honour and authority upon all his countrymen, and for this reason he was much hated by the Greeks.

XIII. When the fortress was fully equipped with every-thing necessary for it, and a countless sum of money § had been deposited there by Illus, he came to the capital (Constantinople) to inform Zênôn that he had executed his will. But Zênôn, because he knew that he was a traitor and was aiming at the soverainty, ordered one of the soldiers to kill him. After the person to whom this commission had been given was for many days seeking an opportunity‖ of executing it secretly, but found none, he accidentally met Illus inside the palace, and drew his sword and raised it to smite him. Instantly, however, one of the soldiers who formed the retinue of Illus struck him

---

* Literally, *camps*.   † The Syriac text has *Basilicus*.

‡ Τὸ Παπούριον καστέλλιν or τὸ Παπουρίου καστέλλιν, which afterwards served as a last refuge for the rebels Illus and Leontius (ch. xvii). See *Theophanis Chronographia*, ed. Classen, vol. i, pp. 196, 201, 203, 204.

§ Literally, *much gold without tale*.

‖ The word ܦܘܪܣܐ is not given in any of the native Syriac lexicons to which I have access, but its meaning is evident from this passage and that in ch. lix.

with a knife on the arm, and the sword fell from his hand and merely cut off Illus's ear. Zênôn, in order that his treachery towards Illus might not be disclosed, at once gave orders that that soldier's head should be cut off, without any inquiry. But this very circumstance only made Illus think the more that Zênôn had ordered him; and he arose and departed thence and went down to Antioch, having made up his mind that, whenever an opportunity offered, he would take measures to requite him.

XIV. Zênôn, being afraid of Illus, because he knew his evil design, despatched to him at Antioch certain men of standing, and sent him word to come up to him (to Constantinople), as if he wished to make excuses to him, pretending that that treachery was not committed at his instigation, but that he did not wish to kill him. However he could not soften the hard heart of Illus; for he despised him, and did not choose to obey his command and go to him. At last Zênôn sent to him another general, whose name was Leontius, with the troops under his orders, and bade him bring Illus up to him by force, and if he offered any resistance even to kill him. When this man arrived at Antioch, he was corrupted by the gold of Illus, and disclosed to him the order which had been given to him to put him to death. And when Illus saw that he had hidden nothing from him, he too showed him a large quantity of gold that he had in his hands, for the sake of which Zênôn was wishing to kill him; and he persuaded Leontius to conspire with him and to rebel along with him, pointing out to him also the hatred of the Greeks towards Zênôn. After he had consented, Illus was able to disclose his design, for alone he could not rebel nor make himself emperor, because the Greeks hated him too on account of his race and of his hardness of heart.

XV. Leontius then became emperor at Antioch in name, whilst Illus was in fact the administrator of affairs. As some say, he was even scheming to kill Leontius, in case they should overcome Zênôn. But there was in their following a certain rascally conjuror, by name Pamprepius *, who confounded and upset all their plans by his perfidy. In order that their throne

---

* Παμπρέπιος. See Lebeau, *Histoire du Bas-Empire*, ed. Saint-Martin, t. vii, p. 132.

might be firmly established, they sent ambassadors to Persia, with a large sum of money, to conclude a treaty of friendship, ... * or, if they required an army to help them, they should send it to them. When Zênôn heard of what had happened at Antioch, he sent thither one of his generals, whose name was John †, with a large army.

XVI. When Illus and Leontius ‡ heard of the great force that was coming against them, their hearts trembled; and the people of Antioch too were afraid that they might not be able to stand a siege, and called on them tumultuously to quit the city, and, if they were able, to meet [John in] battle. This caused Illus and Leontius much anxiety, and they formed plans for quitting Antioch, and crossing the river Euphrates eastwards. And they sent one of their partisans, whose name was Matronianus §, with five hundred horsemen, to establish their authority in Edessa as a seat of government. The Edessenes, however, rose up against him, and closed the gates of the city, and guarded the wall after the fashion of war, and did not let him enter.

XVII. When Illus and Leontius heard this, they were forced to meet John in battle; but they were not strong enough for this, because John fell upon them manfully, and destroyed the greater part of the troops that were with them, while the rest were scattered every man to his city. They themselves, being unable to bear his onslaught, took those that were left with them, and made their escape to the fortress of which I have said above that it was impregnable and well provided with stores of every kind (ch. xii). John pursued after them, but did not overtake them, and encamped around ‖ the fortress and kept watching it. They, because they relied upon the impregnability of the fortress, let the troops that were with them go

---

* The first alternative in their proposal seems to have been accidentally omitted by the scribe.

† John the Scythian. See Lebeau, *op. cit.*, t. vii, p. 138.

‡ Οἱ περὶ (ἀμφὶ) Ἴλλον καὶ Λεόντιον. That in this and similar phrases, here and in the next chapter, Illus and Leontius are chiefly or solely meant, is clear from the words ܘܐܬܩܛܠܘ ܬܪܝܗܘܢ, "both of them were put to death," in ch. xvii. I have translated accordingly.

§ Assemâni writes *Metroninus;* see *Bibliotheca Orientalis*, t. i, p. 264, col. 1.

‖ This translation is not quite exact, a word being illegible in the MS.

down, retaining with them only chosen men and valiant. John appeased his fury upon those who came down from the fortress, but was unable to harm Illus and Leontius in any way. Now because of the difficulty of the natural position of the fortress, it was also rendered wonderfully impregnable by the work of men's hands, and there was no path leading up to it save one, by which, because of its narrowness, not even two persons could ascend at once. However, after a considerable time, when all John's stratagems were exhausted, Illus and Leontius were betrayed by those who were with them, and were taken captive in their sleep. By the order of Zênôn both of them were put to death, as well as those who betrayed them, and the hands of all who were with them were cut off. Such were the troubles of the Greek empire in the days of Pêrôz.

XVIII. After the sudden disappearance of Pêrôz, which I have mentioned above (ch. xi), his brother Balâsh * reigned over the Persians in his place. This was a humble man and fond of peace. He found nothing in the Persian treasury, and his land was laid waste and depopulated by the Huns, (for thou in thy wisdom dost not forget what expense and outlay kings incur in wars, even when they are victorious, and how much more when they are defeated,) and from the Greeks he had no help of any kind such as his brother had. For he sent ambassadors to Zênôn, asking him to send him money; but because he was occupied with the war against Illus and Leontius, and because he also remembered the money that had been sent by them at the commencement of their rebellion, which still remained there in Persia, he did not choose to send him anything, save this verbal message: "The taxes of Nisîbis which thou receivest are enough for thee, which for many years past have been due to the Greeks."

XIX. Balâsh then, because he had no money to maintain his troops, was despised in their eyes. The priesthood † too hated him, because he was trying to abolish their laws, and wishing to build baths (βαλανεῖα) in the cities for bathing ‡;

---

* See Noeldeke, *Gesch. der Perser* u. s. w., p. 133, and *Zeitschrift der D. M. G.*, Bd xxviii, pp. 94, 95.

† ܡܓܘܫܐ, the *Magi*. See Noeldeke, *Gesch. d. Perser* u. s. w., p. 450.

‡ See Noeldeke, *op. cit.*, p. 134, note 5.

and when they saw that he was not counted aught in the eyes of
his troops, they took him and blinded him, and set up in his
stead Ḳawâd *, the son of his brother Pêrôz, whose name we
have mentioned above (ch. x), who was left as a hostage among
the Huns, and who it was that stirred up the war with the
Greeks, because they did not give him money. For he sent
ambassadors, and a large elephant as a present to the emperor,
that he might send him money. But before the ambassadors
reached Antioch in Syria, Zênôn died, and Anastasius became
emperor after him. When the Persian ambassador informed
his master Ḳawâd of this change in the Greek government, he
sent him word to go up with diligence and to demand the
customary money, or else to say to the emperor, "Take war."

XX. And so, instead of speaking words of peace and
salutation, as he ought to have done, and of rejoicing with him
on the commencement of the soverainty which had been newly
granted him by God, he irritated the mind of the believing
emperor Anastasius with threatening words. But when he
heard his boastful language, and learned about his evil conduct,
and that he had reestablished the abominable sect (αἵρεσις) of
the magi which is called that of the Zarâdushtaḳân †, (which
teaches that women should be in common, and that every one
should have connexion with whom he pleases,) and that he had
wrought harm to the Armenians who were under his sway,
because they would not worship fire, he despised him, and did
not send him the money, but sent him word, saying, "As Zênôn,
who reigned before me, did not send it, so neither will I send it,
until thou restorest to me Nisîbis; for the wars are not trifling
which I have to carry on with the barbarians who are called the
Germans, and with those who are called the Blemyes ‡, and with

---

* See Noeldeke, *op. cit.*, p. 135.

† The followers of Mazdak, the son of Bâmdâdh, who was the disciple of
Zarâdusht, the son of Khôragân. See Noeldeke, *Gesch. d. Perser* u. s. w., pp.
455—467, especially pp. 456—7.

‡ Βλέμυες or Βλέμμυες, an Ethiopian or negro race, who used to harry Upper
Egypt. Quatremère, in his *Mémoires géogr. et histor. sur l'Égypte*, t. ii, p. 131,
identified them with the Buja, البجة or البجاة, of the Arabian geographers;
but they seem rather to be the same as the *Beliyûn* (?) of al-Idrîsî, البليون.
See Dozy and De Goeje, *Description de l'Afrique et de l'Espagne par Edrisi*, pp.
٢١, ٢٧, and pp. 26, 32.

many others: and I will not neglect the Greek troops and feed thine."

XXI.   When the Armenians who were under the rule of Ḳawâd heard that he had not received a peaceful answer from the Greeks, they took courage and strengthened themselves, and destroyed the fire-temples that had been built by the Persians in their land, and massacred the magi who were among them. Ḳawâd sent against them a general * with an army to chastise them and make them return to the worship of fire; but they fought with him, and destroyed both him and his army, and sent ambassadors to our emperor, offering to become his subjects.   He however was unwilling to receive them, that he might not be thought to be stirring up war with the Persians. Let those therefore who blame him because he did not give the money, rather blame him who demanded what was not his as if by force; for had he asked for it peaceably and by persuasion, it would have been sent to him; but he hardened his heart like Pharaoh, and used threats of war.   But we place our trust in the justice of God, that He will bring upon him a greater punishment than that of the other because of his filthy laws, for he wished to violate the law of nature and to destroy the path of the fear of God.

XXII.   Next the whole of the Ḳadishâyê † who were under his sway rebelled against him, and wanted to enter Nisîbis, and to set up in it a king of their own; and they fought against it for a considerable time.   The Ṭamûrâyê ‡ too, who dwell in the land of the Persians, when they saw that nothing was given to them by him, rebelled against him.   These placed their trust in the lofty mountains amid which they dwelt, and used to come down and spoil and plunder the villages around them, and (rob) the merchants, both forainers and natives of the place, and then go up again.   The nobles too of his kingdom hated him, because he had allowed their wives to commit adultery.   The

* The word in the original is *marzĕbânâ* or *marzbân*, which signifies in Persian "warden of the marches," or what the Germans call "Markgraf."   It is nearly equivalent to the older term of "satrap."   See Noeldeke, *Gesch. d. Perser* u. s. w., p. 102, note 2, and p. 446.

† They dwelt in the neighbourhood of Sinjâr and Dârâ.   See Noeldeke in the *Zeitschrift d. D. M. G.*, Bd xxxiii, p. 157.

‡ See Noeldeke, *loc. cit.*, p. 158, note 4.

Arabs * also who were under his sway, when they saw the confusion of his kingdom, likewise made predatory raids, as far as their strength permitted, throughout the whole Persian territory.

XXIII. There arose at this time another trouble in the Greek territory also; for the Isaurians, after the death of Zênôn, rebelled against the emperor Anastasius, and were wishing to set up an emperor who was pleasing to themselves †. When Ḳawâd heard this, he thought that he had found his opportunity, and sent ambassadors to the Greek territory, thinking that they would be afraid and would send him money, since the Isaurians had rebelled against them. But the emperor Anastasius sent him word, saying, "If thou askest it as a loan, I will send it to thee; but if as a matter of custom, I will not neglect the Greek armies, which are sore put to it in the war with the Isaurians, and become a helper of the Persians." By these words the spirit of Ḳawâd was humbled, because his plan had not succeeded. The Isaurians were overcome and destroyed and slaughtered, and all their cities were rased and burned. The Persian grandees plotted in secret to slay Ḳawâd, on account of his impure morals and perverse laws; and when this became known to him, he abandoned his kingdom, and fled to the territory of the Huns, to the king at whose court he had been brought up when he was a hostage.

XXIV. His brother Zâmâshp ‡ reigned in his stead over the Persians. Ḳawâd himself took to wife among the Huns his sister's daughter§. His sister had been led captive thither in the war in which his father was slain; and because she was a king's daughter, she became the wife of the king of the Huns, and he had a daughter by her ||. When Ḳawâd fled thither, she gave him this daughter to wife. Being emboldened by having become the king's son-in-law, he used to weep before him every

---

* In the text *Ṭaiyâyê*, which originally designated the Arabs of the tribe of Ṭaiyi', ﻄﻲ , one of the most powerful in northern Arabia.

† See Lebeau, *op. cit.*, t. vii, p. 229 sqq.

‡ See Noeldeke, *Gesch. d. Perser* u. s. w., p. 142 and note 2.

§ See Noeldeke, *op. cit.*, p. 137, note 1.

|| See Noeldeke, *op. cit.*, p. 130, with notes 1 and 3.

day, imploring him to give him the aid of an army, that he
might go and kill the grandees and establish himself on his
throne. His father-in-law gave him a by no means small army,
according to his request. When he reached the land of the
Persians, his brother heard of it, and fled before him, and he
accomplished his wish and slew the grandees. He also sent a
message to the Ṭamûrâyê, threatening them that, if they did
not submit to him of their own accord, they would be conquered
in war; but, if they would join his army, that they should enter
with him the Greek territory, and out of the spoil of that
country he would distribute to them all that had been wrongly
withheld from them (see ch. xxii). They were afraid of the
Hunnish army, and yielded to him. The Ḳadishâyê, who were
encamped against Nisîbis (ch. xxii), when they heard this,
submitted likewise. And the Arabs, when they learned that he
was going to make war with the Greeks, crowded to him with
great alacrity. The Armenians, on the other hand, who were
afraid lest he should take vengeance on them because of those
fire-temples which they had rased in time past, were unwilling
to obey him. But he collected an army and went to war with
them; and though he was too strong for them, he did not
destroy them, but promised them that he would not even
compel them to worship fire, if they would be his auxiliaries in
the war with the Greeks. They consented most unwillingly,
because they were afraid. What things Ḳawâd did after he
entered the Greek borders, I will tell thee hereafter in their
proper time; but just now, as thou hast bidden me to write
unto thee also about the signs and chastisements which took
place, in their due order, and about the locusts and the
pestilence and the dearth, and these are antecedent in point of
time, I will turn my discourse unto them. And that the
narrative may not be confused, I will set down the years
separately, one by one, and under each of them, by and for
itself, I will state what happened in it, God being my helper by
the aid of the prayers of thee His elect.

XXV. *The year of Alexander* 806 (A.D. 494—5). Concerning then the cause of the war, and how it was provoked, I have, as I think, sufficiently informed thee, O our father, though I have written down these narratives in brief terms, because I was anxious to avoid prolixity. Some of them I found in old books; others I learned from meeting with men who had acted as ambassadors to both monarchs; and others from those who were present at these occurrences. But now I am going to inform thee of the things that happened with us, because with this year commenced the violent chastisements and the signs that have taken place in our own days.

XXVI. At this time our bodies were perfectly sound all over, but the pains and diseases of our souls were many. But God, who finds pleasure in sinners when they repent of their sins and live, made our bodies as it were a mirror for us, and filled our whole bodies with sores, that by means of our exterior He might show us what our interior was like unto, and that, by means of the scars of our bodies, we might learn how hideous were the scars of our souls. And as all the people had sinned, all of them were smitten with this plague. For there were swellings and tumours* upon all the people of our city, and the faces of many gathered and became full of matter, and they presented a horrid sight. There were some whose whole bodies were full of boils or pustules, down even to the palms of their hands and the soles of their feet; whilst others had large holes in their several limbs. However, by the goodness of God which protected them, the pain did not last long with any one, nor did any defect or injury result in the body; but, though the scars of the sores were quite plain after healing, the limbs were preserved in such a state as to fulfil their functions in the body. At this time thirty modii of wheat were sold at Edessa for a dînâr, and fifty of barley†.

XXVII. *The year* 807 (A.D. 495—6). On the 17th of Îyâr (May) in this year, when blessings were sent down

---

* The word ܝܩܕܢܐ is explained in the native glossaries by خَرَاجَات.

† ܩܘܡܕܝ is the Latin *modius*. By ܕܝܢܪ, dînâr (the Latin *denarius*), is here meant the Byzantine *aureus*.

abundantly from heaven upon all men, and the crops by the
blessing (of God) were abundant, and rain was falling, and the
fruits of the earth were growing in their season, the greater part
of the citizens (of Edessa) cut off all hope of safety for their lives
by sinning openly.   Being plunged in all sorts of luxurious
pleasures, they did not even send up thanks for the gifts of
God, but were neglectful of [this duty], and corrupted by the
diseases of sins.   And as if the secret and open sins in which
they were indulging were not enough for them, they were
present on the day above specified, that is to say, on the night
between the Friday and Saturday*, [at the place] where the
dancer (ὀρχηστής) who was named Trimerius was dancing †.
They kindled lamps without number in honour of this festival,
a custom which was previously unknown in this city.   These
were arranged by them on the ground along the river‡ from the
gate of the Theatre§ as far as the gate of the Arches‖.   They
placed on its bank lighted lamps (κανδήλαι), and hung them in
the porticoes (στοαί), in the town-hall¶, in the upper streets**,

---

* Literally, *which is the day of Friday, the dawning of the Saturday.*

† See the note on the Syriac text.

‡ The Daiṣân, ܕܝܨܢ, or Ḳara Ḳoyûn, which now flows round the northern
part of the city, but in ancient times ran right through it from N.W. to S.E.,
parallel to, or perhaps coinciding with, the modern 'Ain al-Khalîl or 'Ain
Ibrâhîm.

§ This was apparently on the eastern side of the city, at the exit of the
Daiṣân.

‖ So I have ventured to translate the word, reading it ܚܛܐ, plural of

ܚܛܬܐ. See Cureton, *Ancient Syriac Documents*, p. ܩܡܗ, l. 22. But my

friend Professor G. Hoffmann, of Kiel, reads ܠܬܪܥܐ ܕܚܛܐ, "to the gate of

the Grottoes" or "Tombs," meaning thereby the grottoes or tombs cut out in the
range of heights to the west of the city. At any rate, this gate lay on the west
side of the city, at or near the entrance of the Daiṣân.

¶ Ὁ ἀντίφορος, the town-hall (perhaps so called from its being situated *ante
forum*). See Procopius, *De Aedificiis*, ii. 7, ed. Dindorf, t. iii, p. 229.

** If the conjecture ܫܘܩܐ ܥܠܝܐ be right, the "upper streets" are
those in the S.W. corner of the city, where there is a hill, on which lay the old
town (ܟܒܐ) of king Abgâr with its buildings and fortifications. See the account
of the great flood, A. Gr. 513, A. D. 201, in Assemâni, *Bibl. Orient.*, t. i, pp. 390—3.
The reading of the MS. is, however, very uncertain. Originally it seems to have

and in many (other) places. Because of this wickedness a marvellous sign was wrought by God to reprove them. For the symbol of the Cross, which the statue (ἀνδριάς -άντα) of the blessed emperor Constantine held in its hand, receded from the hand of the statue about one cubit, and remained thus during the Friday and Saturday until evening. On the Sunday the symbol came of its own accord and drew nigh to its place, and the statue took it in its hand, as it had held it before. By means of this sign the discreet understood that the thing that had been done was very far removed from what was pleasing unto God.

XXVIII. *The year* 808 (A.D. 496—7). This sign from above was not sufficient for us to restrain us from our sins; on the contrary, we became more audacious, and gave ourselves up easily to sins. The small slandered their neighbours, and the great were full of respect of persons. Envy and treachery prevailed among all of us; and adultery and fornication abounded. The plague of boils became more prevalent among the people, and the eyes of many were destroyed both in the city and the (surrounding) villages. Mâr Cyrus* the bishop displayed a seemly zeal, and exhorted the citizens to make a small litter† of silver in honour of the eucharistic vessels, that they might be placed in it when they were going to minister with them at the commemoration of one of the martyrs. Every one gave according to his means, but Eutychianus, the husband of Aurelia‡, was the first to show right good will, giving a hundred dînârs of his own property.

XXIX. Anastasius the governor (ἡγεμών) was dismissed, and Alexander came in his place at the end of this year. He cleared the streets of the city of filth, and swept away the

---

had]ܠܬܐ ܣܩܒܐ, which was subsequently altered into]ܩܒܐ. If

]ܠܬܐ ܣܩܒܐ be correct, it would seem to mean "the corn-market"

(]ܠܬܐ =]ܠܬܐ).

* *Mâr*, shortened from *Mârî*, means "my lord."

† Λεκτίκιον, *lectica*. The word is feminine in Syriac, like ܣܡܐ? from δημόσιον.

‡ *Aurelia* is only a conjectural emendation. See the note on the Syriac text. Assemâni gives *Irene, Bibl. Orient.*, t. i, p. 267, col. 2.

booths* which had been built by the artisans in the porticoes
and streets. He also placed a box ($\kappa\iota\beta\omega\tau\delta$s) in front of his
palace ($\pi\rho\alpha\iota\tau\omega\rho\iota\nu$), and made a hole in the lid of it, and wrote
thereon, that, if any one wished to make known anything, and
it was not easy for him to do so openly, he should write it down
and throw it into it without fear. By reason of this he learned
many things which many people wrote down and threw into it.
He used to sit regularly every Friday in the church† of S. John
the Baptist and S. Addai the Apostle, and to settle legal causes
without any expense. And the wronged took courage against
their wrongers, and the plundered against their plunderers, and
brought their causes before him, and he decided them. Some
causes which were more than fifty years old, and had never been
inquired into, were brought before him and settled. He con-
structed the covered walk ($\pi\epsilon\rho\iota\pi\alpha\tau$os -ov)‡, which was beside
the gate of the Arches§. He began also to build the public bath
($\delta\eta\mu\delta\sigma\iota\nu$), which had been planned years before to be built
beside the granary|| of corn. He gave orders that the artisans
should hang over their shops on the eve of Sunday¶ crosses
with five lighted lamps ($\phi\alpha\nu\iota$) attached to them.

XXX. *The year* 809 (A. D. 497—8). Whilst these things
were taking place, there came round again the time of that
festival at which the heathen tales were sung; and the citizens
(of Edessa) took even more pains about it than usual. For
seven days previously they were going up in crowds to the

* , or more commonly , , plural of
 or , in Arabic , , in later Hebrew
, , perhaps ultimately from $\sigma\tau\iota\beta\alpha$s -$\delta\alpha$, $\sigma\tau\iota\beta\delta\iota\nu$.

† , $\mu\alpha\rho\tau\iota\rho\iota\nu$, a church in which the relics of a saint or saints
are preserved.

‡ In Byzantine writers $\pi\epsilon\rho\iota\pi\alpha\tau$os means *a rampart* (see Du Cange), but here
the word appears to bear its older sense of *covered walk, cloister*. Martin,
however, renders the word by "un Paropton," and adds: "$\pi\alpha\rho\delta\pi\tau\nu$ désignait,
à proprement parler, la pièce de bain nommée le *Calidaire*."

§ See above, p. 18, note ||.

|| The MS. reads , which may be derived from $\sigma\iota\tau\iota\kappa\delta$s, or may
perhaps be an error for , $\sigma\iota\tau\omega\nu$ -$\omega\nu\alpha$, $\sigma\iota\tau\omega\nu\iota\nu$.

¶ I. e., on the night between Saturday and Sunday.

theatre at eventide, clad in linen garments, and wearing turbans*, with their loins ungirt. Lamps (κανδῆλαι) were lighted before them, and they were burning incense, and holding vigils the whole night, walking about the city and praising the dancer† until morning, with singing and shouting and lewd behaviour (στρῆνος). For these reasons they neglected also to go to prayer, and not one of them bestowed a thought on his duty, but in their pride they mocked at the modesty of their fathers, who, quoth they, "did not know how to do these things as we do"; and they kept saying that the inhabitants of the city in the olden times were simpletons and fools (ἰδιῶται). In this way they became daring in their impiety, and there was none to warn or rebuke or admonish. For although Xenaias, the bishop (ἐπίσκοπος) of Mabbôg‡, was at the time in Edessa,— of whom beyond all others it was thought that he had taken upon him to labour in teaching,—yet he did not speak with them on this subject more than one day. But God in His mercy showed them clearly the care which He had for them, that they might be restrained from their iniquity. For the two colonnades (βασιλικαί) and the tepidarium (or lukewarm-bathroom)§ of the summer bathhouse fell down; but by God's goodness nobody was hurt there, although many people were at work in it both inside and outside, and no one perished of them except two men, who were crushed, as they were fleeing from the noise of the fall, at the door of the coldwater-bathroom.

* ܦܩܝܠܐ is not ποικιλά, embroidered robes, but φακιόλια (φακεόλια, φακεωλίδες), a kind of turbans. See Du Cange.

† Probably Trimerius (see ch. xxvii). Unless we should read ܐܪܩܘܕܐ, the dancers.

‡ Mabbôg or Mabûg, Hierapolis, now Membij, ܡܢܒܓ. On Xenaias or Philoxenus, the friend of Severus, patriarch of Antioch, see Assemâni, Bibl. Orient., t. ii, p. 10, and Bickell, Conspectus rei Syrorum literariae, p. 40. Also Wright, Catalogue of Syriac MSS. in the British Museum, p. 526, sqq.

§ So Martin has plausibly rendered the words ܒܝܬ ܩܪܝܪܐ. The MS. however has ܒܝܬ ܩܪܝܪܐ; and it is possible that we should read ܒܝܬ ܡܝܬܐ, the urinal or latrine. From ܡܝܬܐ, urina, is derived the Arabic medical term تفسرة.

Whilst they were laying hold of it from opposite sides, to make it revolve, they were delayed by this struggle as to which of them should get out first, and the stones fell upon them and they died. All sensible men gave thanks to God that He had preserved the city from having to mourn for many; for this bath was to have been opened* in a few days. So complete was its downfall that even the lowest ranges of stone, which were laid on the surface of the ground, were uprooted from their places.

XXXI. In this same year was issued an edict of the emperor Anastasius that the money should be remitted which the artisans used to pay once in four years †, and that they should be freed from the impost. This edict was issued, not only in Edessa, but in all the cities of the Greek empire. The Edessenes used to pay once in four years one hundred and forty pounds of gold ‡. The whole city rejoiced, and they all put on white garments, both small and great, and carried lighted tapers (κηρίωνες) and censers full of burning incense, and went forth with psalms and hymns, giving thanks to God and praising the emperor, to the church of S. Sergius and S. Simeon, where they celebrated the eucharist. They then reentered the city, and kept a glad and merry festival during the whole week, and enacted that they should celebrate this festival every year. All the artisans were reclining and enjoying themselves, bathing, and feasting § in the court of the (great) Church ‖ and in all the porticoes of the city.

---

* This is merely a *quid pro quo.* If ﻞﺴﻤﺋ be correct, it can only mean that "this bath was to have let (people) bathe in a few days."

† The tax called χρυσάργυρον. See Lebeau, *op. cit.*, t. vii, p. 247.

‡ ﻼﻤﻠ, λίτραι, *librae*. The word was used by the Phoenicians of Sardinia in the second century B.C. (*Sard. triling.* 1, מאת לטרם משקל), and still survives in Arabic in the shape of *riṭl* or *raṭl,* رِطْل.

§ The word rendered "feasting," ﻤﺴﻤﻨ, means literally "reclining" (or, as we should say, "sitting") at table. The word translated "bathing" was very doubtful in the MS., and has now altogether disappeared.

‖ By "the Church" *par excellence* we are, I suppose, to understand "the great Church of S. Thomas the Apostle" (see Assemâni, *Bibl. Orient.*, t. i, p. 399). It is uncertain, however, whether the actual reading of the manuscript is not ﻼﺜﻋﺩ ﻼﺜﺼ, "in the courts of the churches."

XXXII. In this year, on the 5th of the month of Khazîrân (June), Mâr Cyrus the bishop departed this life, and Peter succeeded him *. He added to the festivals of the year that of Palm Sunday. He also established the custom of consecrating the water on the night immediately preceding the feast of the Epiphany; and he prayed † over the oil of unction on the Thursday (in Passion Week) before the whole people; besides regulating the other feasts. Alexander the governor was dismissed, and Demosthenes succeeded him. By his order all the porticoes of the city were whitewashed, whereat persons of experience were much annoyed, for they said that it was a warning sign of approaching evils that were to befal their home ‡.

XXXIII. *The year* 810 (A.D. 498—9). A proof of God's justice was manifested towards us at this time, for the correction of our evil conduct; for in the month of Îyâr (May) of this year, when the day arrived for the celebration of that wicked heathen festival, there came a vast quantity of locusts into our country from the south. They did not, however, destroy or harm anything in this year, but merely laid their eggs § in our country in no small quantity. After their eggs were deposited in the ground, there were terrible earthquakes in the land; and it is clear that they took place to awaken the people out of the sin in which they were plunged, that they might not be (further) chastised by famine and pestilence.

XXXIV. In the month of Âb (August) of this year there came an edict from the emperor Anastasius that the fights of wild beasts in the amphitheatre (κυνήγιον) should be suppressed in all the cities of the Greek empire. In the month of Îlûl (September) there was a violent earthquake, and a great sound was heard from heaven over the land, so that the earth trembled from its foundations at the sound; and all the villages and towns heard that sound and felt the earthquake. Alarm-

---

* See Le Quien, *Oriens Christianus*, t. ii, col. 962. This Cyrus was the second bishop of the name.

† The word rendered "he prayed" was uncertain in the MS., and has now wholly vanished.

‡ The text is uncertain, but this is no doubt the general sense of the passage.

§ Literally, "planted."

ing rumours and evil reports came to us from all quarters; and, as some said, a marvellous sign was seen in the river Euphrates and at the hotspring of Abarnê *, in that the water which flowed from their fountains was dried up this day. It does not appear to me that this is false, because, whenever the earth is rent by earthquakes, it happens that the running waters in those places that are cleft are restrained from flowing, and are at times even turned into another direction; as the blessed David too, when telling in the eighteenth psalm † of the punishments that came from God upon His enemies, by means of the shaking of the earth and the cleaving of the mountains, and the like, lets us know that this also took place. For he says ‡: "The fountains of the waters were laid bare, and the foundations of the world were seen, at Thy rebuke, O Lord." There came too in the course of this month a letter, which was read in church before the whole congregation, stating that Nicopolis § had fallen to the ground of a sudden at midnight and overwhelmed all its inhabitants. Some strangers (ξένιοι) too who were there, and certain brethren from our schools (σχολαί) who were travelling thither and happened to be on the spot, were buried (in the ruins). Their companions who came (back from thence) told us (this). The whole wall of the city all round, and everything that was within it, was overturned in that night, and not one person of them remained alive, save the bishop of the town and two other men, who were sleeping behind the apse (κόγχη) of the altar of the church. When the ceiling of the room in which they were sleeping fell, one end of its beams was propped up by the wall of the altar, and so it did

---

* See Land, *Anecdota Syriaca*, t. ii, p. 210, l. 7. The hotspring of Abarnê lies near Chermûk or Chermîk, چرميك, northwards of ܣܘܡܝܣܛܐ or Süverek, midway between the Euphrates and Tigris. See Ammianus Marcellinus, 18, 9, 2, and J. J. Benjamin II, *Eight Years in Asia* (Hanover, 1863), p. 82. I owe these references to Professor G. Hoffmann. The reading ܕܐܒܪ̈ܢܝܐ ܣܘܥܣܐ, "the hotspring of the Iberians (Georgians)" is indefensible. It occurs also, however, in the *Chronicon Edessenum*, as edited by Assemâni, *Bibl. Orient.*, t. i, p. 406, no. lxxvi.

† Psalm xviii. 7, sqq.   ‡ Psalm xviii. 15.

§ Another name for Emmaus, عموأس, in Palestine, about halfway between Jaffa and Jerusalem.

not bury them. A certain brother, whose veracity can be depended upon, has told me as follows. "At eventide of the night when Nicopolis fell, we were lying down inside the town, I and a companion of mine. He was very restless, and said to me, 'Get up, and let us go and pass the night outside of the town in yonder cave, as is our custom, for I cannot get rest here, because the air is so sultry and sleep will not come to me.' So we got up, I and he, and went out of the town, and passed the night in the cave, as was our custom. When the time of dawn drew nigh, I awakened the brother who was with me, and said to him, 'Get up, for it is daybreak, and let us go into the town, and attend to our business.' So we got up, I and he, and came into the town, and found all its houses overturned, and the people and the cattle, the oxen and the camels, buried therein; and the sound of their groaning was coming up from under the ground. Those who came together to the spot took out the bishop from beneath the beams (of the roof) by which he was sheltered. He asked for bread and wine, wherewith to celebrate the eucharist, [but could get none,] because the whole town was overturned and nothing in it left standing. Presently, however, there arrived a wayfarer, a good man, who gave him some small pieces of bread and a little wine, and he celebrated the eucharist and prayed, and made those who were there participate in the mystery of life. He resembled at this time, as it seems to me, the just Lot when he made his escape from Sodom." Thus much is sufficient to tell.

XXXV. Again, in the north there was a church called that of Arsamosata *, which was very strongly built and beautifully decorated. On a fixed day in each year, namely on the day of the commemoration of the martyrs who were deposited in it, many used to gather together thither from all quarters, partly for prayer and partly for traffic; for great provision was made for the people who were assembled on that occasion. When there was a great crowd collected of men and women and children, of

---

* The name of Ἀρσαμόσατα, in Arabic شِمْشَاط, Shimshât, is pronounced in Syriac Arshemshât, which is represented in Greek letters by Ἀρχημχάτ or Ἀρχιμχάτ (see Wright's Catalogue, p. 433, col. 2). It lay in the district of Khartabirt or Kharput, eastwards of that place.

every age and class, there were terrible flashes of lightning and
violent peals of thunder and frightful noises; and all the people
fled to the church, to seek refuge with the bones of the saints.
And whilst they were in great fear, and were engaged in prayer
and service at midnight, the church fell in and crushed beneath
it the greater part of the people who were in it.   This happened
on the same day on which Nicopolis fell.

XXXVI. *The year* 811 (A.D. 499—500).   By all these
earthquakes and calamities, however, not a man of us was
restrained from his evil ways, so that our country and our city
remained without excuse.   Because we had been preserved
from the chastisement inflicted on others *, and rumours from
afar had not alarmed us, we were (presently) smitten with a
stroke for which there was no healing.   Let us recognise therefore the justice of God and say, "Righteous is the Lord, and
very upright are His judgments†;" for lo, in His longsuffering
He was yet willing by means of signs and wonders to restrain
us from our evil doings.   In the month of the first Teshrîn
(October) of this year, on the 23d, which was a Saturday, at the
rising of the sun, his brightness was taken away from him,
and his sphere of light appeared like silver.   He had no per-
ceptible rays, and our eyes could easily gaze upon him without hindrance, for he had neither rays nor beams to hinder
them from looking upon him.   Just as it is easy for us to
look upon the moon, so we could look upon him.   He continued
thus till towards the eighth hour.   The ground over which
shone the little light that there was, seemed as if ashes or
sulphur had been sprinkled upon it‡.   On this day another
dreadful and terrible sign took place on the wall of the city.
This city, which, because of the faith of its king and the
righteousness of its inhabitants in days of old, was deemed
worthy to receive a blessing from our Lord (see ch. v), was well
nigh overwhelming its inhabitants at the present day, because
of the multitude of their sins.   For there was a breach in the
wall from the south to the Great Gate§; and some of the

---

* Following the correction suggested in the note on the Syriac text.
† Psalm cxix. 137.
‡ In what terms would Joshua have described a dense London fog?
§ The Great Gate lay at the S.E. corner of the town, leading out to Ḥarrân.

stones at this spot were scattered to no inconsiderable distance from it. By the order of our father the bishop Mâr Peter, public prayers were offered, and every one besought mercy from God. He took all his clergy (κλῆρος) and all the members of religious orders, both men and women, and all the lay members of the holy Church, both rich and poor, men women and children, and they traversed all the streets of the city, carrying crosses, with psalms and hymns, clad in black garments of humiliation. All the convents too in our district kept up continual services with great diligence; and so, by the prayers of all the holy ones, the light of the sun was restored to its place, and we were a little cheered.

XXXVII. In the latter Teshrî (November) we saw three signs in the sky at midday *. One of them was in the midst of the heavens in the south. It resembled in its colour the bow that is in the clouds, and with its concave surface it looked upwards; that is to say, its convex surface was downwards and its extremities were upwards. And there was one on the east, and another also on the west. Again, in the latter Kânûn (January), we saw another sign in the exact southwest corner (γωνία) (of the heavens) †, which resembled a spear. Some people said of it that it was the besom of destruction, and others said that it was the spear of war.

XXXVIII. Till now we were chastised (only) with rumours and signs; but for the future who is able to tell of the affliction that surrounded our land on all sides? In the month of Âdâr (March) of this year the locusts came upon us out of the ground, so that, because of their number, we imagined that not only had the eggs that were in the ground been hatched to our harm, but that the very air was vomiting them against us, and that they were descending from the sky upon us. When they were only able to crawl, they devoured and consumed all the Arab territory and all that of Râs-'ain ‡ and Tellâ § and Edessa.

* Apparently *parhelia* or mock suns.

† Literally, *on the south and west, in the very corner.* A comet is probably meant.

‡ Rîsh-'ainā, 'Ρέσαινα, in Arabic رأس عَيْن.

§ ܛܶܠܐ ܕܡܰܘܙܰܠܬܐ or تل مَوزَن, called by the Greeks *Constantia* or

But after they were able to fly, the stretch of their radii was from the border of Assyria to the Western Sea (the Mediterranean), and they went northwards as far as the boundary of the Ôrtâyê *. They ate up and desolated these districts and utterly consumed everything that was in them, so that, even before the war broke out, we could see with our own eyes what was said of the Babylonian †, "The land is as the garden of Eden before him, and behind him a desolate wilderness." Had not the providence of God restrained them, they would have devoured human beings and cattle, as we have heard that they actually did in a certain village, where some people had put down a little baby in a field, while they were working; and before they got from one end of the field to the other, the locusts leaped upon it and deprived it of life. Presently after, in the month of Nîsân (April), there began to be a dearth of corn and of everything else, and four modii of wheat were sold for a dînâr. In the months of Khazîrân (June) and Tammûz (July) the inhabitants of these districts were reduced to all sorts of shifts to live. They sowed millet for their own use, but it was not enough for them, because it did not thrive. Before the year came to an end, misery from hunger had reduced the people to beggary, so that they sold their property for half its worth, horses and oxen and sheep and pigs. And because the locusts had devoured all the crop, and left neither pasture nor food for man or beast, many forsook their native places and removed to other districts of the north and west. And the sick who were in the villages, as well as the old men and boys and women and infants, and those who were tortured by hunger, being unable to walk far and go to distant places, entered into the cities to get a livelihood by begging; and thus many villages and hamlets (*agûrsâ, ἀγρός*) were left destitute of inhabitants. They did not, however, escape punishment, not

---

Constantina, between Mâridîn and Edessa, westwards of Deyrik or Dêrik, at the place called Vêrânshehr.

* The inhabitants of the district of Anzêtênê, whose chief town was Ἀνζῆτα, ܐܢܙܝܛ or ܐܢܙܝܛ, هَنْزِيط, in the south of Armenia. See Noeldeke in the *Zeitschrift der D. M. G.*, Bd xxxiii, p. 163.

† Joel, ch. ii. 3.

even those who went to far off places; but, as it is written
concerning the Children of Israel *, "Whithersoever they went
out, the hand of the Lord was against them for evil," so also it
fared with them; for the pestilence came upon them in the
places to which they went, and even overtook those who
entered into Edessa; about which I shall tell (thee) presently
to the best of my ability, though no one, as I think, is able
to describe it as it really was.

XXXIX. Now, however, I am going to write to thee about
the dearth, as thou didst ask me. I did not, it is true, wish to
set down anything regarding this, but I have constrained
myself to do so, that thou mightest not think that I treated
thy order slightingly. Wheat was sold at this time at the rate
of four modii for a dînâr, and barley six modii. Chickpeas
were five hundred nûmia† a ḳab‡; beans, four hundred nûmia
a ḳab; and lentils, three hundred and sixty nûmia a ḳab; but
meat was not as yet dear. As time went on, however, the
dearth became greater, and the pain of hunger afflicted the
people more and more. Everything that was not edible was
cheap§, such as clothes and household utensils and furniture, for
these things were sold for a half or a third of their value (τιμή),
and did not suffice for the maintenance of their owners, because
of the great dearth of bread. At this time our father Mâr
Peter set out to visit the emperor (at Constantinople), in order
to beg him to remit the tax (συντέλεια, capitatio). The
governor ||, however, laid hold of the landed proprietors¶, and

---

* Judges, ch. ii. 15.

† The Syriac word is ܩܘܡܝܐ, which may either be the plural of ܩܘܡܐ,
νοῦμμος, nummus, or the word νούμιον itself. Hence too, in all probability, the
form ܠܘܡܐ, ܠܘܡܐ.

‡ κάβος, from the Hebrew קַב, = χοῖνιξ.

§ ܩܘܡܐ is explained in Bar-Bahlûl's lexicon, and Hoffmann's *Opuscula
Nestoriana*, p. 84, l. 1, by ܐܪܙܝ, i.e. Pers. أرْزَان, and Arabic رخيص, *cheap*.

|| ܕܝܢܐ, *the judge*, here = ܗܓܡܘܢܐ, ἡγεμών.

¶ ܩܘܡܐ ܡܪ̈ܐ, the Pers. Arab. دهاقين, *the dihḳâns*, regarding whom
see Noeldeke, *Gesch. d. Perser u. s. w.*, p. 351, note 1, and p. 440.

used great violence to them and extorted it from them, so that, before the bishop could persuade the emperor, the governor had sent the money to the capital. When the emperor saw that the money had arrived, he did not like to remit it; but, in order not to send our father away empty, he remitted two folles* to the villagers, and the price which they were paying†, whilst he freed the citizens from the obligation of drawing water for the Greek soldiery‡.

XL. The governor himself too set out to visit the emperor, girt with his sword§, and left Eusebius to hold his post and govern the city. When this Eusebius saw that the bakers were not sufficient to make bread for the market, because of the multitude of country people, of whom the city was full, and because of the poor who had no bread in their houses, he gave an order that every one who chose might make bread and sell it in the market. And there came Jewish women, to whom he gave wheat from the public granary (ἀπόθετον), and they made bread for the market. But even so the poor were in straits, because they had not money wherewith to buy bread; and they wandered about the streets and porticoes and court-yards to beg a morsel of bread, but there was no one in whose house bread was in superfluity. And when one of them had begged (a few) pence, but was unable to buy bread therewith, he used to purchase therewith a turnip or a cabbage (κράμβη) or a mallow (μαλάχιον, μολόχιον), and eat it raw. And for this reason there was a scarcity of vegetables, and a lack of every-thing in the city and villages, so that people actually dared to enter the holy places and for sheer hunger to eat the con-secrated bread as if it had been common bread. Others cut pieces off dead carcases, that ought not to be eaten, and cooked and ate them; to which things thou in thy truthfulness canst bear testimony.

---

* ܩܠܣ, i.e. φόλλις, follis, Arab. فُلْس fuls, or فَلْس fals. See Noeldeke in the *Z. d. D. M. G.*, Bd xxxv, p. 497.

† There is evidently some error or omission here in the text.

‡ So I translate the word ܪܗܘܡܝܐ in this passage, for ܪܗܘܡܝܐ frequently means nothing more than *a (Roman or Greek) soldier*.

§ To show that he was still in office, and had not been deposed.

XLI. *The year* 812 (A. D. 500—1). In this year, after the vintage, wine was sold at the rate of six measures for a dînâr, and a ḳab of raisins for three hundred nûmia. The famine was sore in the villages and in the city; for those who were left in the villages were eating bitter-vetches, and others were frying the withered fallen grapes* and eating them, though even of them there was not enough to satisfy them. And those who were in the city were wandering about the streets, picking up the stalks and leaves of vegetables, all filthy with mud, and eating them. They were sleeping in the porticoes and streets, and wailing by night and day from the pangs of hunger; and their bodies wasted away, and they were in a sad plight, and became like jackals because of the leanness of their bodies. The whole city was full of them, and they began to die in the porticoes and in the streets.

XLII. After the governor Demosthenes had gone up to the emperor, he informed him of this calamity; and the emperor gave him no small sum of money to distribute among the poor. And when he came back from his presence to Edessa, he sealed many of them on their necks with leaden seals, and gave each of them a pound of bread a day. Still, however, they were not able to live, because they were tortured by the pangs of hunger, which wasted them away. The pestilence became worse about this time, namely the month of the latter Teshrî (November); and still more in the month of the first Kânûn (December), when there began to be frost and ice, because they were passing the nights in the porticoes and streets, and the sleep of death came upon them during their natural sleep. Children and babes were crying † in every street.

---

* ܩܣܛܝܣ evidently does not mean here "grapestones," but the small withered grapes that had fallen from the vines before attaining maturity; according to the glossaries, ما يَسقُط من العِنَب او من الكَرْم ويَجِفّ

, or more briefly, التَحَشُّف في مَوضِعه او يَجِفّ في كَرْمه ويَسقُط من العِنَب.

† The Syriac word ܦܥܐ, פְּעָא, expresses the *bleating* of sheep. Compare פָּעָה in Isaiah, ch. xlii. 14.

Of some the mothers were dead ; others their mothers had left, and had run away from them, when they asked for something to eat, because they had nothing to give them. Dead bodies were lying exposed in every street, and the citizens were not able to bury them, because, whilst they were carrying out the first that had died, the moment that they returned, they found others. By the care of Mâr Nonnus, the ξενοδόχος *, the brethren used afterwards to go about the city, and to collect these dead bodies. And all the people of the city used to assemble at the gate of the ξενοδοχεῖον, and go forth and bury them, from morning to morning. The stewards of the (Great) Church, the priest Mâr Tĕwâth-îl† and Mâr Stratonîcus (who some time afterwards was deemed worthy of the office of bishop in the city of Harrân‡), established an infirmary§ among the buildings attached to the (Great) Church of Edessa. Those who were very ill used to go in and lie down there ; and many dead bodies were found in the infirmary§, which they buried along with those at the ξενοδοχεῖον.

XLIII. The governor blocked up‖ the gates of the colonnades (βασιλικαί) attached to the winter bath (δημόσιον), and laid down in it straw and mats, and they used to sleep there, but it was not sufficient for them. When the grandees of the city saw this, they too established infirmaries, and many went in and found shelter in them. The Greek soldiers too set up places in which the sick slept, and charged themselves with their expenses. They died by a painful and melancholy death ; and though many of them were buried every day, the number still went on increasing. For a report had gone forth through-

---

* The Syriac word ‏ܟܣܢܕܟܪܐ‎ is formed by putting the Latin termination *arius* to the Greek word in the text. The Syrians added the same appendage to a Persian word, ‏ܐܣܛܘܢܐ‎ a *pillar*, ‏ܐܣܛܘܢܪܐ‎ a *stylite*; and even to the native word ‏ܐܠܦܐ‎, a *boat* or *ship*, whence ‏ܐܠܦܪܐ‎, a *boatman* or *sailor*.

† Assemâni *Bibl. Orient.*, t. i, p. 271, col. 2, writes *Tutaël*, ‏ܬܘܬܐܝܠ‎, on what authority I do not know.

‡ See Le Quien, *Oriens Christ.*, t. ii, col. 977.

§ See the notes on the Syriac text, chapters xlii and xliii.

‖ In the native glossaries the word ‏ܣܟܪ‎ is explained by ‏ܣܛܡ‎ and ‏ܐܣܕ‎.

out the province of Edessa, that the Edessenes took good care
of those who were in want; and for this reason a countless
multitude of people entered the city. The bath ($\beta\alpha\lambda\alpha\nu\epsilon\hat{\imath}o\nu$)
too that was under the Church of the Apostles*, beside the
Great Gate†, was full of sick, and many dead bodies were carried
forth from it every day. All the inhabitants of the city were
careful to attend in a body the funeral of those who were
carried forth from the $\xi\epsilon\nu o\delta o\chi\epsilon\hat{\imath}o\nu$, with psalms and hymns and
spiritual songs that were full of the hope of the resurrection.
The women too (were there) with bitter weeping and loud
cries. And at their head went the diligent shepherd Mâr
Peter; and with them too was the governor, and all the nobles.
When these were buried, then every one came back, and
accompanied the funeral of those who had died in his own
neighbourhood. And when the graves of the $\xi\epsilon\nu o\delta o\chi\epsilon\hat{\imath}o\nu$ and
the Church were full, the governor went forth and opened the
old graves that were beside the church of Mâr Kônâ‡, which
had been constructed by the ancients with great pains, and
they filled them. Then they opened others, and they were not
sufficient for them; and at last they opened any old grave, no
matter what, and filled it. For more than a hundred bodies
were carried out every day from the $\xi\epsilon\nu o\delta o\chi\epsilon\hat{\imath}o\nu$, and many a
day a hundred and twenty, and up to a hundred and thirty,
from the beginning of the latter Teshrî (November) till the end
of Âdâr (March). During that time nothing could be heard in
all the streets of the city but either weeping over the dead or
the lamentable cries of those in pain. Many too were dying in
the courts of the (Great) Church, and in the courts of the city
and in the inns§: and they were dying also on the roads, as
they were coming to enter the city. In the month of Shĕbâṭ
(February) too the dearth was very great, and the pestilence

---

* See Assemâni, *Bibl. Orient.*, t. i, p. 403, lines 8—13.

† See above, p. 26, note §.

‡ Κόνος or Κοῦνος, or perhaps Κόνων, bishop of Edessa, who died in, or soon
after, A. Gr. 624 = A.D. 312—13. See Assemâni, *Bibl. Orient.*, t. i, p. 271, col. 2;
p. 393, no. xii; p. 424, no. i; Le Quien, *Oriens Christ.*, t. ii, col. 955.

§ Or *khâns*. The word ܦܢܕܩܐ comes from the Greek πανδοκεῖον, πανδο-
χεῖον, in Arabic فندق, whence in Spanish *fonda*, but also *alhondiga*, Ital.
fondaco.

J. S.   *e* increased. Wheat was sold at the rate of thirteen ḳabs for a dînâr, and barley eighteen ḳabs. A pound of meat was a hundred nûmia, and a pound of fowl three hundred nûmia, and an egg forty nûmia. In short there was a dearth of everything edible.

XLIV. There were public prayers in the month of Âdâr (March) on account of the pestilence, that it might be restrained from the strangers (ξένιοι); and the people of the city, while interceding on their behalf, resembled the blessed David when he was saying to the Angel who destroyed his people *, "If I have sinned and have done perversely, wherein have these innocent sheep sinned? Let thy hand be against me and against my father's house." In the month of Nîsân (April) the pestilence began among the people of the city, and many biers were carried out in one day, but no one could tell their number. And not only in Edessa was this sword of the pestilence, but also from Antioch as far as Nisîbis the people were destroyed and tortured in the same way by famine and pestilence. Many of the rich died, who were not starved; and many of the grandees too died in this year. In the months of Khazîrân (June) and Tammûz (July), after the harvest, we thought that we might now be relieved from dearth. However our expectations were not fulfilled as we thought, but the wheat of the new harvest was sold so dear as five modii for a dînâr.

XLV. *The year* 813 (A.D. 501—2). After these afflictions of locusts and famine and pestilence, about which I have written to thee, a little respite was granted us by the mercy of God, that we might be able to endure what was to come, as we learned from the actual facts. There was an abundant vintage, and wine from the press was sold at the rate of twenty-five measures for a dînâr; and the poor were amply supplied from the vineyards by means of the crop of dried grapes. For the husbandmen and farmers said that the crop of dried grapes was more abundant than that of wheat, because there was a hot wind when the grapes began to ripen, and the greater part of them dried up. By the discreet it was said that this took place by the good providence of God, the Lord of all, and that this thing was a mingling of mercy with chastisement, that the

* 2 Samuel, ch. xxiv. 17.

villagers might be supported by this supply of dried grapes, and not die of hunger as in the past year; because at this time wheat was sold at the rate of only four modii for a dînâr, and barley six modii. During the two Teshrîs (October and November) there was the following sign of mercy. The whole winter of this year was excessively rainy; and the seed that was sown shot up here and there to more than the height of a man, before the month of Nîsân (April) was come. Even barren spots of land produced nearly as much as those that were sown. The very roofs of the houses produced much grass, which some people reaped and sold like the dog's grass * of the fields; and because it had spikes and was of the full height, the buyers did not perceive (the difference). We were expecting and hoping this year too that corn would be very cheap †, as in the years of old; but our hopes came to nought, for in the month of Îyâr (May) there blew a hot wind for three days, and all the corn of our land was dried up save in a few places.

XLVI. In this month, when the day came on which the wicked festival of the tales of the (ancient) Greeks ‡ was held, of which we have spoken above, there came an edict from the emperor Anastasius that the dancers (ὀρχησταί) should not dance any more, not even in a single city throughout his empire. Any one, therefore, who looks to the issue of things, will not blame us because of our having said that, by reason of the wickedness which the people of the city perpetrated at this festival, the chastisements of hunger and pestilence came upon us in succession. For, behold, within thirty days after it was abolished, wheat, which had been sold at the rate of four modii for a dînâr, was sold at the rate of twelve; and barley, which had been sold at the rate of six, was sold at the rate of twenty-two. And it was clearly made known to every one, that the will of God is able to bless a small crop, and to give abundance to those who repent of their sins; for although the whole crop of grain was dried up, as I have said, yet from the little remnant that was left came all this relief within thirty days. Perhaps,

---

* ܟܣܘܣ, probably ἄγρωστις, *triticum repens* or "dog's grass", اَلشِّيَل.

† See p. 29, note §.

‡ Of course ܝܘ̈ܢܝܐ, *the Ionians*, not ܪ̈ܗܘܡܝܐ, *the Byzantines*.

however, even now some one may say that I have not reasoned well, for this repentance was in no wise a voluntary one, that mercy should be shown for it, seeing that it was the emperor who abolished the festival by force, in that he ordered that the dancers should not dance at all. We, on the contrary, say that God, because of the multitude of His goodness, was seeking an occasion to show mercy even unto those who were not worthy. Of this we have a proof from the fact that He had mercy upon Ahab, when he was put to shame by the rebuke of Elijah, and did not bring in his days the evil which had been before decreed against his house *. I do not, however, by any means assert that this was the only sin which was perpetrated in our city, for many were the sins that were wrought secretly and openly; but because the rulers too participated in them, I do not choose to specify these sins distinctly, that I may not give occasion to those who like it of finding fault and of saying of me that I speak against the chiefs. That I may not, however, leave the matter in complete obscurity,—because I promised above to make known unto thee whence this war was stirred up against us,—and that I may not moreover say aught against the offenders, I will (merely) set down the words of the Prophet, from which thou mayest understand (my meaning), who, when he saw his fellow-citizens committing acts like these which are this day committed in our city, especially where you live, and throughout the whole province (χώρα), said unto them as if from the mouth of the Lord †: "Woe unto him that saith to the father, What begettest thou? and to the woman, Wherewith travailest thou?" About other matters it is better to be silent, for it is fitting to hearken to the passage of Scripture which says ‡: "Let him that is prudent keep silence in that time, because it is a time of evil." But if our Lord grants that we see thee in health, we will speak with thee of these things according as we are able.

XLVII. Now then listen to the calamities that happened in this year, and to the sign that appeared on the day when they happened, for this too thou hast required at my hands. On the 22d of Âb (August) in this year, on the night preceding

---

* 1 Kings, ch. xxi. 29.   † Isaiah, ch. xlv. 10.
‡ Amos, ch. v. 13.

Friday*, a great fire appeared to us blazing in the northern quarter the whole night, and we thought that the whole earth was going to be destroyed that night by a deluge of fire; but the mercy of our Lord preserved us without harm. We received, however, a letter from some acquaintances of ours, who were travelling to Jerusalem, in which it was stated that, on the same night in which that great blazing fire appeared, the city of Ptolemais or 'Akkô † was overturned, and nothing in it left standing. Again, a few days after, there came unto us some Tyrians and Sidonians, and told us that, on the very same day on which the fire appeared and Ptolemais was overturned, the half of their cities fell, namely of Tyre and Sidon. In Bêrŷtus (Beirût) only the synagogue of the Jews fell down on the day when 'Akkô was overturned. The people of Nicomedia (in Bithynia) were delivered over to Satan to be chastised, and many of them were tormented by demons, until they remembered the words of our Lord ‡, and persevered in fasting and prayer, and received healing.

XLVIII. On the very same day on which that fire was seen, Ḳawâd, the son of Pêrôz, the king of the Persians, collected the whole Persian army, and went up against the north. He entered the Greek territory with the force of Huns that he had with him, and encamped against Theodosiûpolis of Armenia §, and took it in a few days; for the governor of the place, whose name was Constantine, rebelled against the Greeks, and surrendered it, because of some enmity that he had against the emperor. Ḳawâd consequently plundered the city, and destroyed and burned it; and he laid waste all the villages in the region of the north, and the fugitives that were left he carried off captive. Constantine he made one of his generals, and left a garrison in Theodosiûpolis, and marched thence.

---

* We would say, "on Thursday night." This display of the *aurora borealis* must have been unusually magnificent.

† In Arabic عكّا, corrupted by us and the French into *Acre*.

‡ S. Matthew, ch. xvii, 21.　　§ أرزن الرُّوم, *Erzerûm*.

XLIX. *The year* 814 (A.D. 502—3). On the region of Mesopotamia also, in which we dwell, great calamities weighed heavily in this year, so that the things which Christ our Lord decreed in His Gospel against Jerusalem, and actually brought to pass, and the things too which have been spoken regarding the end of this world, would be well fitting to those which befel us at this time. For after there had been earthquakes in various places, as I have written unto thee, and famines and pestilences, and alarms and terrors, and after great signs had been shown from heaven, nation arose against nation and kingdom against kingdom, and we fell by the edge of the sword, and were led away captive into every region, and our land was trampled under foot by strange nations; so that, had it not been for the words of our Lord, who has said *, " When ye hear of wars and tumults, be ye not afraid, for these things must needs first come to pass, but the end is not yet come," we would have dared to say that the end of the world *was* come, because many thought and said thus. But we ourselves reflected that this war did not extend over the *whole* world; and besides we remembered too the words of S. Paul, wherewith he warned the Thessalonians † concerning the coming of our Lord, saying that they should not be astonied either by word, or by spirit, or by beguiling epistle, as if it were from him, declaring the day of the Lord to be now come; and (how) he showed that it is not possible that the end should be until the false Christ is revealed. From these words then of our Lord and of His Apostle we understood that these things did not befal us because it was the latter time, but that they took place for our chastisement, because our sins were great.

L. Ḳawâd, the king of the Persians, came from the north on the fifth of the first Teshrî (October), on a Saturday, and encamped against the city of Âmid, which is beside us in Mesopotamia, he and his whole army. When Anastasius, the Greek emperor, heard that Ḳawâd had collected his forces, he was unwilling to meet him in battle, that blood might not be shed on both sides; but he sent him money by the hand of Rufinus, to whom he gave orders that, if Ḳawâd was on the frontier and had not yet crossed over into the Greek territory,

* S. Matthew, ch. xxiv. 6.   † 2 Thessalonians, ch. ii. 2, 3.

he should give him the money and send him away. But when
Rufinus came to Caesarea of Cappadocia, and heard that
Kawâd had laid waste Agêl* and Ṣûph† and Armenia and the
Arabs‡, he left the money at Caesarea, and went to him, and
told him that he should recross the border and take the money.
He however would not, but seized Rufinus and ordered him to
be kept under guard. He fought against Âmid, he and his
whole army, with every manner of warfare, by night and by
day, and built against it (the mound called) a mule§; but the
people of Âmid built and added to the height of the wall.
When the mule was raised high, the Persians applied the
battering-ram ‖; and after they had struck the wall violently,
the part newly built became loosened, because it had not yet
settled, and fell. But the Âmidenes dug a hole in the wall
under the mule, and secretly drew away inside the city the
earth which was heaped up to form it, propping it up with
beams as they worked; and so the mule collapsed and fell.

LI. When Kawâd found that he was not a match for the
city, he sent Naʿmân,¶ the king of the Arabs (of al-Ḥîrah), with
his whole force, to go southwards to the district of Ḥarrân**.
Some of the Persian troops advanced as far as the city of

* ﺍﻧﺠﻞ, ’Αγγιληνή, أنجل, Egil or Enjil, north of Diyâr-bekr.

† ﺻﻮﻑ, the people of which are ﺻﻮﻓﻨﺎ, Σωφηνή or Σωφανηνή,
adjacent to Agêl.

‡ Meaning here the most northern of the nomade Arabs of Mesopotamia,

§ In Syriac ﻗﻮﻣﺘﺎ, a huge mound of earth, which Procopius (de bello
Persico, I. 7) calls λόφος.

‖ Literally, "the ram's head."

¶ The Arabs write the name النعمان, an-Noʿmân, and some Syriac authors
too give ﻧﻌﻤﻦ. The person in question is an-Noʿmân III, ibn al-Aswad,
who reigned from A.D. 498 to 503. See Caussin de Perceval, Essai sur l'histoire
des Arabes, t. ii, p. 67, and Reiske, Primae lineae historiae regnorum Arabicorum,
ed. Wüstenfeld, p. 42.

** חָרָן, ﺣﺮﺍﻥ, Χαρράν, Χαρρά, Κάρρα, Κάρραι, Carrae, still retains its ancient
name of ﺣﺮﺍﻥ, Ḥarrân.

Constantina or Tellâ*, and were plundering and harrying and laying waste the whole country. On the 19th of the latter Teshrî (November) Olympius†, the dux‡ of Tellâ, and Eugenius, the dux of Melitênê§ (who had come down at that time), went forth, they and their troops, and destroyed the Persians whom they found in the villages around Tellâ. And when they had turned to go back to the city, some one told them that there were five hundred men in a ravine not very far from them. They were ready to go against them, but the Greek troops that were with them had dispersed themselves to strip the slain; and because it was night, Olympius gave orders to light a fire on the top of an eminence and to blow trumpets, that those who were scattered might rejoin them. But the Persian generals, who were encamped at the village of Tell Beshmai‖, when they saw the light of the fire and heard the sound of the trumpets, armed all their force and came against them. When the Greek cavalry saw that the Persians were too many for them, they turned (their backs); but the infantry were unable to escape and were constrained to fight. So they came together and drew up in battle array, forming what is called the χελώνη or tortoise, and fought for a long time. But as the army of the Persians was too many for them, and there were added to these the Huns and Arabs, their ranks were broken, and they were thrown into disorder, and mixed up among the cavalry, and trampled and crushed under the hoofs¶ of the horses of the Arabs. So many of the Greeks were killed, and the rest were made prisoners.

LII. On the 26th of this month Naʿmân came from the south and entered the territory of the Ḥarrânites, and laid waste and plundered and took captive the people and cattle

---

* See above, p. 27, note §.

† Some authorities call him Alypius, which would be written in Syriac ܐܠܘܦܝܘܣ.

‡ Δούξ = ἡγεμών, ἄρχων. See Du Cange.

§ Now Malaṭyah, مَلَطِيَّة.

‖ Tell Beshmai or Tell Besmai, تَل بِسْمَة, west of Mâridîn, near Deyrik or Dêrik.

¶ The Syriac text has *in the dust*, ܒܥܦܪܐ.

and property of the whole territory of Ḥarrân. He came also as far as Edessa, harrying and plundering and taking captive all the villages. The number of persons whom he led away into captivity was 18,500, besides those who were killed, and besides the cattle and property and spoil of all kinds. The reason that all these people were found in the villages was its being the time of the vintage, for not only did the villagers go out to the vintage, but also many of the Ḥarrânites and Edessenes went out, and were taken prisoners. Because of these things Edessa was closed and guarded, and ditches* were dug, and the wall was repaired; and the gates of the city were stopped up† with blocks of stone, because they were decayed. They were going to put new ones, and to make bars ($\mu o\chi\lambda o\acute{\iota}$) for the sluices ($\kappa\alpha\tau\alpha\rho\rho\acute{\alpha}\kappa\tau\alpha\iota$) of the river, lest any one should enter thereby‡; but they could not find iron enough for the work, and an order was issued that every house in Edessa should furnish ten pounds of iron. When this was done, the work was finished. When Eugenius saw that he could not meet all the Persians (in battle), he took what troops were left him, and went against the garrison which they had at Theodosiûpolis, and destroyed those who were in it, and retook the town.

LIII. Ḳawâd was still fighting against Âmid, and striving and labouring to set up again the mule that had fallen in §. He ordered the Persians to fill it up with stones and beams, and to bring cloths of hair and wool and linen, and make them into bags‖ or sacks, and fill them with earth, and pile them up on the mule which they had made, so that it might be raised quickly against the wall. Then the Âmidenes constructed

---

* ܩܘܣܐ, φόσσαι, fossae. Hence الفسطاط, i. e. τὸ φοσσάτον or φωσσάτον. See Du Cange.

† See p. 32, note ‖.

‡ At this time the Daiṣân ran through the city, not round it. See above, p. 18, note ‡; and compare Assemâni, *Bibl. Orient.*, t. i, p. 391, l. 7.

§ See ch. l, at the end.

‖ ܡܠܟܐ is explained in the native glossaries by كيس، مسح، جوالق,

and شليف, which last is of course borrowed from the Syriac.

a machine which the Persians named "the Crusher"*, because it thwarted all their labour and destroyed themselves. For the Âmidenes cast with this engine huge stones, each of which weighed more than three hundred pounds; and so the cotton awning under which the Persians concealed themselves was rent in pieces, and those who were standing beneath it were crushed. The battering ram too was broken by the constant shower of stones which were cast without cessation; for the Âmidenes were not able to damage the Persians so much in any other way as by means of large stones, because of the cotton awning which was folded many times over (the mule). Upon this the Persians used to pour water, and it could neither be damaged by arrows on account of its thickness, nor by fire because it was damp. But these large stones that were hurled from "the Crusher" destroyed both awning and men and weapons. In this way the Persians were discomfited, and gave up working at the mule, and took counsel to return to their own country, because, during the three months that they had sat before it, 50,000 of them had perished in the battles that were fought daily both by night and day. But the Âmidenes became over-confident in their victory, and fell into careless ways, and did not guard the wall with the same diligence as before. On the 10th of the month of the latter Kânûn (January) the guardians of the wall drank a great deal of wine because of the cold, and when it was night, they fell asleep and were sunk in a heavy slumber; and some of them quitted their posts, because it was raining, and went down to seek shelter in their houses. Whether then through this remissness, as we think, or by an act of treachery, as people said, or as a chastisement from God, the Persians got possession of the walls of Âmid by means of a ladder, without the gates being opened or the wall breached. They laid waste the city, and sacked all the property in it, and trampled the eucharist under foot, and mocked at its service, and stripped bare its churches, and led its inhabitants into

---

* ܠܩܘܼܫܵܐ is a pure Syriac formation from the radical ܚܒܫ, מָבַח, ܛܒ݂ܓ; but the writer probably thought of the Persian word *tôpâh*, "ruin, destruction, injury, mischief", in later times تبأ, *tabâh*.

captivity, except the old and the maimed and those who hid
themselves. They left there a garrison of three thousand men,
and all (the rest) of them went down to the mountains of
Shîgâr*. That the Persians who remained might not be
annoyed by the smell of the dead bodies of the Âmidenes, they
carried them out and piled them up in two heaps outside of the
north gate. The number of those who were carried out by the
north gate was more than 80,000; besides those whom they led
forth alive and stoned outside of the city, and those whom they
stabbed on the top of the mule that they had constructed, and
those who were thrown into the Tigris (Deḳlath), and those who
died by all sorts of deaths, regarding which we are unable
to speak.

LIV. Then Ḳawâd let Rufinus go, that he might go and
tell the emperor what had been done; and he was speaking of
these atrocities everywhere, and by these reports the cities to
the east of the Euphrates were alarmed, and (their inhabitants)
made ready to flee to the west. The honoured Jacob †, the periodeutes, who has composed many homilies on passages of the
Scriptures, and written various poems and hymns regarding the
time of the locusts, was not neglectful at this time too of his
duty, but wrote letters of admonition to all the cities, bidding
them trust in the Divine deliverance, and exhorting them not
to flee. The emperor Anastasius too, when he heard this, sent a
large army of Greek soldiers to winter in the cities and garrison
them. All the booty that he had taken, and the captives that
he had carried off, were not, however, enough for Ḳawâd, nor
was he sated with the great quantity of blood that he had shed;
but he (again) sent ambassadors to the emperor, saying,

---

* Shîgâr or Shiggâr, Σίγγαρα, Σίγγαρα, Arab. سِنْجَار Sinjâr.

† Jacob, at present periodeutes or visitor, afterwards bishop of Baṭnân
(Βάτναι, Batnae) in Sĕrûg, سَروج, one of the most prolific of Syriac writers. He
died A. Gr. 833 (A.D. 521). See Assemâni, *Bibl. Orient.*, t. i, p. 283 sqq.;
Abbeloos, *De vita et scriptis S. Jacobi Sarugensis;* Matagne in the *Acta
Sanctorum* for October, t. xii, p. 824, with the supplement, p. 927; Bickell,
Conspectus rei Syrorum literariae, p. 25. Compare also Wright, *Catalogue of the
Syriac MSS. in the Brit. Mus.*, p. 502 sqq. The volume Add. 14,587, contains
several of the letters referred to in the text; *op. cit.*, p. 518 sqq. On the word
περιοδευτής, in Syriac ܦܪܝܘܕܘܛܐ, see Du Cange.

"Send me the money or accept war." This was in the month of Nîsân (April). The emperor, however, did not send the money, but made preparations to avenge himself and to exact satisfaction for those who had perished. In the month of Îyâr (May) he sent against him three generals, Areobindus ('Αρεόβινδος), Patricius, and Hypatius, and many officers with them*. Areobindus went down and encamped on the border by Dârâ and 'Ammûdîn †, towards the city of Nisîbis; he had with him 12,000 men. Patricius and Hypatius encamped against Âmid, to drive out thence the Persian garrison; they had with them 40,000 men. There came down too at this time the hyparch ‡ Appion §, and dwelt at Edessa, to look after the provisioning of the Greek troops that were with them. As the bakers were not able to make bread enough, he ordered that wheat should be supplied to all the houses of Edessa and that they should make soldiers' bread ‖ at their own cost. The Edessenes turned out at the first baking 630,000 modii.

LV. When Ḳawâd saw that those who were with Areobindus were few in number, he sent against them the troops that he had with him in Shîgâr, (namely) 20,000 Persians; but Areobindus routed them once and again, until they were driven to the gate of Nisîbis, and many of the fugitives were suffocated at the gate as they were pressing to get in. In the month of Tammûz (July) the Huns and Arabs joined the Persians to come against him, with Constantine (see ch. xlviii) at their head. When he learned this from spies, he sent Calliopius the Aleppine to Patricius and Hypatius, saying, "Come to me and help me, because a large army is about to come against me." They, however, did not listen to him, but stayed where they were beside Âmid. When the Persians came against the army of Areobindus, he could not contend with them, but left his camp, and made his escape to Tellâ and Edessa; and all their baggage ¶ was plundered and carried off.

* See Lebeau, *op. cit.*, t. vii, p. 354.

† Τὸ 'Αμμώδιος χωρίον, Ammodia, 'Amûdîyah, southwestwards from Dârâ.

‡ Commissary-general, χορηγὸς τῆς τοῦ στρατοπέδου δαπάνης. See Du Cange.

§ See Lebeau, *op. cit.*, t. vii, p. 356.

‖ βουκελλάτον, βουκελάτον, *buccellatum*. See Du Cange.

¶ This must be the meaning of the word ܚܨ݂ܐ in this passage; very similar to ܚܨ݂ܐ, עוֹבָדְתָּא.

LVI. The troops of Patricius and Hypatius were (mean-while) constructing three towers of wood, wherewith to scale the walls of Âmid. But when they had finished building the towers at a great expense, and they were girded with iron so as not to be harmed by anything, then they found out what had happened on the frontier, and they burned the towers, and de-parted thence, and went after the Persians but did not overtake them. One of the officers, whose name was Pharazmân*, and another named Theodore †, sent by stratagem a flock of sheep to pass by Âmid, while they and their troops lay in ambush. When the Persians saw the sheep from within Âmid, about four hundred chosen men of them sallied forth to carry them off; but the Greeks who were lying in ambush arose and destroyed them, and took their leader alive. He promised them that he would give up Âmid to them, and for this reason Patricius and Hypatius returned thither; but when that general was unable to fulfil his promise, because those in the city would not be persuaded by him, the generals ordered him to be impaled.

LVII. The Arabs of the Persian territory advanced as far as the Khâbûr ‡, and Timostratus the dux (δούξ) of Callinîcus §, went out against them and routed them. The Arabs of the Greek territory also, who are called the Tha'labites ‖, went to Ḥîrtâ ¶

---

* See Lebeau, *op. cit.*, t. vii, p. 355.   † *Ibid.*, pp. 343, 357.

‡ نصّدزا, Χαβώρας, Ἀβώρας, etc., اَلْخَابُور.

§ The same as ar-Rakkah, اَلرَّقَّة.

‖ The Benû Tha'labah, بْنُو ثَعْلَبَة, the leading branch of the great tribe of Bekr ibn Wâïl (Wüstenfeld, *Tabellen*, 2te Abth., B, C), who, in alliance with the southern tribe of Kindah (*ibid.*, 1ste Abth., 4), occupied a large portion of the Syrian desert, between the kingdom of al-Ḥirah on the east and that of the Ghassânides on the west. They were ruled over by the kings of Kindah, of the house of Âkil al-morâr, and the reigning king at this time was al-Ḥârith ibn 'Amr. See Lebeau, *op. cit.*, t. vii, p. 250; Caussin de Perceval, *Essai sur l'histoire des Arabes*, t. ii, p. 69; Reiske, *Primae Lineae*, p. 98; and above all the sketch by my lamented friend Dr. O. Loth, at p. 10 of the pamphlet entitled "*Otto Loth. Ein Gedenkblatt für seine Freunde.* 1881."

¶ ܠܙ̈ܪ, ܠ̈ܝܪܐ, الحِيرَة, al-Ḥirah, the chief town of the petty kingdom of the Lakhmite Arabs. See Caussin de Perceval, *Essai sur l'histoire des Arabes*, t. ii, p. 1 sqq.; Reiske, *Primae Lineae*, p. 25 sqq. It lay within a few miles of the more modern town of al-Kûfah.

(the capital) of Naʿmân, and found a caravan which was going up to him, and camels that were carrying up to him......* They fell upon them and destroyed them and took the camels, but they did not make any stay at al-Ḥîrah, because its inhabitants had withdrawn into the inner desert †. Again, in the month of Âb (August), the whole Persian army assembled, along with the Huns and the Ḳadishâyê and the Armenians, and came against Ôpadnâ ‡. Patricius and his troops heard of this, and arose to go against them; but while the Greeks were yet on the march, and not drawn up for battle, the Persians met the vanguard and smote them. When these who were beaten fell back, the rest of the Greek army saw that the vanguard was smitten, and fear fell upon them, and they did not wait to fight, but Patricius himself was the first to turn, and all his army after him. They crossed the Euphrates, and made their escape to the city of Shĕmîshâṭ §. In this battle Naʿmân too, the king of the Persian Arabs, was wounded. One of the Greek officers, whose name was Peter, fled to the castle of Ashparîn ‖; and when the Persians surrounded the castle, the inhabitants were afraid of them, and gave him up to them, and the Persians took him away prisoner. They slew the Greek soldiers who were with him, but the people of the castle they did not harm in any way.

LVIII. Ḳawâd, the king of the Persians, was thinking of going against Areobindus to Edessa; for Naʿmân, the king of

---

* The word in the Syriac text, if correctly written, is wholly unknown to me; but it is evidently the name of some valuable commodity.

† This seems to be the meaning of the Syriac; literally, "because it had entered into the inner desert." I suspect that the whole sentence is corrupt.

‡ Noeldeke has identified this place with الفُدَين, al-Fudain, which is described by Yâkût in his معجم البلدان as being "a village on the bank of the Khâbûr, between Mâkisîn and Ḳarḳisiyâ (Κιρκήσιον), where a battle was fought." But Hoffmann thinks that the place meant is τὸ ᾿Απάδνας of Procopius (de Aedificiis, ii. 4), which he is inclined to identify with Tell Âbâd, N.W. of Kafr Jôz in Ṭûr ʿAbdîn.

§ ܫܡܝܫܛ, Σαμόσατα, ܫܡܝܫܘܛ.

‖ Τὸ Σίφριος χωρίον or κάστρον ῎Ισφριος, Siphris or Syfreas. See Saint-Martin's note in Lebeau, op. cit., t. vii, p. 359. It must have been situated near Dêrik and Tell Besmeh.

the Arabs, kept urging him on because of what had happened
to his caravan (see ch. lvii). But a shaikh from Ḥîrtâ of
Na'mân, who was a Christian, answered and said : "Let not
your majesty take the trouble of going to war against Edessa,
because there is the infallible word of Christ, whom we worship,
regarding it, that no enemy shall ever make himself master of
it" (see ch. v). When Na'mân heard this, he threatened that
he would do at Edessa worse things than had been done at
Âmid, and uttered blasphemous words. And Christ showed a
manifest sign in him, for at the very time when he blasphemed,
the wound which he had received on his head swelled, and his
whole head became swollen, and he arose and went to his tent,
and lingered in this pain for two days and died *. Not even
this sign, however, restrained the wicked mind of Ḳawâd from
his evil purpose; but he set up a king in place of Na'mân,
and arose and went to battle. When he came to Tellâ, he
encamped against it; and the Jews who were there plotted to
surrender the city to him. They dug a hole in the tower of
their synagogue, which had been committed to them to guard,
and sent word to the Persians regarding it that they might dig
into it (from the outside) and enter by it. This was found out
by the count (κόμης, comes) Peter, who was in captivity (see ch.
lvii), and he persuaded those who were guarding him to let him
come near the wall, saying that there were clothes and articles
of his of different kinds which he had left in the city, and
he wished to ask the Tellenes to give them to him. The
guards granted his request and let him go near. He said to the
soldiers who were standing on the wall to call the count
Leontius, who at that time had charge of the city, and they
called him and the officers. Peter spoke with them in Greek,
and disclosed to them the treachery of the Jews. In order that
the matter might not become known to the Persians, he asked
them to give him a pair of trousers †. They at first made a
pretence of being angry with him; but afterwards they threw

---

* Of erysipelas, the natural result of his wound and of exposure or
excitement.

† Compare in Arabic زَوجُ نِعالٍ , a pair of sandals; وَرِجْلُ سَراوِيلَ
a pair of trousers.

down to him from the wall a pair of trousers, because in reality
he had need of clothes to wear.   Then they went down from
the wall, and as if they had learned nothing about the treachery
of the Jews and did not know which was the place, they went
round and examined the foundations of the whole wall, as if
they wished to see whether it required strengthening.   This
they did for the sake of Peter, lest the Persians might become
aware that he had disclosed the thing and might treat him
much worse.   At last they came to the place which the Jews
were guarding, and found that it was mined, and that they had
made ready in the centre of the tower a great hole, as they had
been told.   When the Greeks saw what was there, they sallied
out against them with great fury, and went round the whole
city, and killed all the Jews whom they could find, men and
women, old men and children.   This they did for (several)
days, and they would scarcely cease from killing them at the
order of the count Leontius and the entreaty of the blessed
Bar-hadad * the bishop.   They guarded the city carefully by
night and by day, and the holy Bar-hadad himself used to
go round and visit them and pray for them and bless them,
commending their care and encouraging them, and sprinkling
holy water † on them and on the wall of the city.   He also
carried with him on his rounds the eucharist, in order to let
them receive the mystery at their stations, lest for this reason
any one of them should quit his post and come down from the
wall.   He also went out boldly to the king of the Persians
and spoke with him and appeased him.   When Ḳawâd saw
the dignified bearing of the man, and perceived too the vigil-
ance of the Greeks, it seemed to him of no use to remain
idle before Tellâ with all that host which he had with him;
firstly, because sustenance could not be found for it in a district that had already been ravaged; and secondly, because
he was afraid lest the Greek generals might join one another
and come against him in a body.   For these reasons he
moved off quickly towards Edessa, and encamped by the river

---

* Βαραδάτος or Βαράδοτος, equivalent to the biblical בֶּן־הֲדַד, Ben-Hădad.
See Lebeau, *op. cit.*, t. vii, p. 363; Le Quien, *Oriens Christ.*, t. ii, col. 968.
   † Literally, "the water of (*i.e.*, used in) baptism."

Gallâb *, otherwise called (the river) of the Medes, for about wenty days.

LIX. Some of the more daring men in his army traversed the district and laid it waste. On the 6th of Îlûl (September) the Edessenes pulled down all the convents and inns that were close to the wall, and burned the village of Kĕphar Sĕlem †, also called Negbath. They cut down all the hedges of the gardens and parks that were around, and felled the trees which were in them. They brought in the bones of all the martyrs (from the churches) which were around the city; and set up engines on the wall, and tied coverings of haircloth over the battlements ‡. On the 9th of this month Ḳawâd sent a message to Areobindus, that he should either receive into the city his general (*marzĕbân*), or come out to him into the plain, as he wished to conclude a treaty of peace with ·him. He gave secret orders however to his troops that, if Areobindus allowed them to enter the city, they should turn and seize the gate and entrance §, until he could come and enter after them; and that, if he came forth to them, they should lie in ambush for him and carry him off alive and bring him to him. But Areobindus, because he was afraid to allow them to enter the city, went forth to them outside, without going very far from the city, but (only) as far as the

---

* In Arabic جلّاب, *Jullâb*. It lies to the E. of Edessa, and runs south-wards into the Balîkh, receiving the Daiṣân or Kara Ḳoyûn from the right a little below Ḥarrân. It is not quite certain whether ܕܡܕܝ really means "of the Medes."

† I.e., "the village of the statue." Its exact site is not known to me, but it must have lain to the E. of the city, not far from the walls.

‡ Martin gives ܟܬܢ̈ܐ, both here and in ch. lxxvi, at the end; but in both cases the manuscript has ܟܬܢ̈ܐ, which bears the same relation to ܟܬܢ̈ܐ that צְאֱצָאִים does to the root יצא. How easily the error could arise, we may see from a manuscript glossary in the India Office, which gives us

ܟܬܢ̈ܐ (*sic*) الشُّرَافات, immediately followed by ܟܡܬܢ̈ܐ ܠܚܡ ܟܬܢ̈ܐ بانياس, to which a later hand has added on the margin شَرَف السُّور ܟܬܢ̈ܐ. The Cambridge MS. of Bar-Bahlûl's lexicon exhibits a further corruption, viz. ܟܬܢ̈ܐ.

§ This would be the ܬܪܥ ܪܒܐ or Great Gate, at the S.E. corner of the city.

J. S.   *g*

church of S. Sergius. There came to him Bâwî *, who was the
asṭabîd †, which is, being interpreted, the magister (militum) ‡
of the Persians, and said to Areobindus, "If thou wishest to
make peace, give us 10,000 pounds of gold, and make an
agreement with us that we shall receive every year the
customary sum of money." Areobindus promised to give as
much as 7,000 pounds, but they would not accept it, and
kept wrangling with him from morning until the ninth hour.
And since they found no opportunity for their treachery, on
account of the Greek soldiers who were guarding him, and
because they were afraid to make war again with Edessa in
consequence of what had happened to Naʿmân, they left Areobindus at Edessa, and went to fight against Ḥarrân, whilst they
sent all the Arabs to Sĕrûg. But the Rîfite § who was in
(command of) Ḥarrân sallied forth secretly from the city, and
fell upon them, and slew of them sixty men, and took alive the
chief of the Huns. As this was a man of mark, and in great
honour with the king of the Persians, he promised the Ḥarrânites that he would not make war upon them, if they would give
him up alive; and they were afraid to fight and gave up that
Hun, sending along with him as a present to him fifteen
hundred rams and other things.

---

* Perhaps, however, ܟܐܘ may be identical with the Persian name بويه,
Buwaih, well known in later Muḥammadan history.

† ܐܣܦܒܕ is the Syriac corruption of the old Persian title *spahpat*,
"master of the soldiery", of which the Greeks have made ἀσπεβέδης, and the
Arabs أصبهبذ. See Noeldeke's *Gesch. der Perser* u. s. w., p. 444, with the
passages referred to in the Index.

‡ Μάγιστρος, *magister*, by itself commonly denotes the majordomo of the
palace or chief officer of the royal household, παλατίου μάγιστρος, called μάγιστρος
τῶν βασιλικῶν ὀφφικίων, who was really τῶν ἐν παλατίῳ ταγμάτων ἀρχηγός. Here
however the term, as explanatory of ܐܣܦܒܕ, seems rather to denote the
magister militum in the East, στρατηγὸς τῆς ἕω or στρατηλάτης Ἀνατολῆς.

§ The MS. has ܪܝܦܐ, the *Rifites*, but the context favours the singular
ܪܝܦܐ, the *Rifite*. This personage seems to be otherwise unknown. Probably
he was an Arab by race, for ܪܝܦܐ seems to be = الرِّيفِي, an adjective formed
from الرِّيف, *the low-lying, cultivated lands along a river*.

LX. The Persian Arabs, who had been sent to Sĕrûg, went as far as the Euphrates, laying waste and taking captive and plundering all that they could. Patriciolus *, one of the Greek officers, with his son Vitalianus, came at this time from the west to go down to the war; and he was confident and fearless, because he had not as yet been in the neighbourhood of the things that had previously happened. When he crossed the River †, he met one of the Persian officers and fought with him and destroyed all the Persians that were with him. Then he set his face to go to Edessa; but he heard from the fugitives that Ḳawâd had surrounded the city, so he recrossed the river and stopped at Shĕmîshâṭ (Samosata). On the 17th of this month, which was Wednesday, we saw the words of Christ and His promises to Abgâr (see ch. v) really fulfilled. For Ḳawâd collected his whole force, and marched from the river Euphrates, and came and encamped against Edessa. His camp extended from the church of SS. Cosmas and Damianus ‡, past all the gardens and the church of S. Sergius § and the village of Bĕkîn ‖, as far as the church of the Confessors ¶; and its breadth was as far as the steep descent of Ṣerrîn **. This whole host

* Patricius, the son of Aspar, a Goth. See Lebeau, *op. cit.*, t. vii, p. 354, at the foot.   † The Euphrates, הַנָּהָר.

‡ Probably situated outside of the gate of Beth-Shĕmesh, ⲀⲙⲢ ⲈⲒⲬⲌⲀⲒ ⲒⲬⲌⲀⲒ, at the N.E. corner of the city. See Assemâni, *Bibl. Orient.*, t. i, p. 405, no. lxviii.

§ This church probably lay some distance S.E. of that of SS. Cosmas and Damianus.

‖ This village must have been S. or S.E. of the church of S. Sergius. I do not know the correct pronunciation of the name. Assemâni gives ⲃⲟⲭⲉⲛ *Bochen*, Martin *Bokeïn*, both mere guesses.

¶ See Assemâni, *Bibl. Orient.*, t. i, p. 395, no. xviii. It lay outside of the ⲒⲬⲌⲀⲒ ⲀⲙⲢ ⲈⲒ ⲬⲌⲀⲒ, on the heights southwest of the town. This gate was on the south side, west of the Great Gate, close to the Karkhâ of Abgâr.

** Assemâni writes *Soren* ⲥⲟⲣⲉⲛ, Martin *Tsareïn*, but the name of صرّين occurs elsewhere, and we have the analogy of صفّين, ⲥⲉⲫⲉⲛ. Professor Hoffmann identifies this ⲥⲟⲣⲉⲛ with *Sürün*, called in some maps *Sermin*, on the right bank of the Germish-chai river, as one goes from the Great Gate to Tellâ and Mâridin.

without number surrounded Edessa in one day, besides the
pickets which it had left on the hills and rising grounds (to the
west of the city). In fact the whole plain (to the E. and
S.) was full of them. The gates of the city were all standing
open, but the Persians were unable to enter it because of the
blessing of Christ. On the contrary, fear fell upon them, and
they remained at their posts, no one fighting with them, from
morning till towards the ninth hour. Then some went forth
from the city and fought with them; and they slew many
Persians, but of them there fell but one man. Women too
were bearing water, and carrying it outside of the wall, that
those who were fighting might drink; and little boys were
throwing stones with slings. So then a few people who had
gone out of the city drove them away and repulsed them
far from the wall, for they were not farther off from it than
about a bowshot; and they went and encamped beside the
village of Ḳubbê *.

LXI. Next day Areobindus too went forth outside of the
Great Gate; and while he was standing opposite the Persian
army, he sent word to Ḳawâd, saying, "Now thou seest by
experience that the city is not thine, nor of Anastasius, but
it is the city of Christ, who blessed it, and has withstood
thy hosts, so that they cannot become masters of it." Ḳawâd
sent word to him, saying, "Give me hostages ($\ddot{o}\mu\eta\rho o\iota$) that
ye will not come out after me when I have struck my camp
to depart; and send me those men whom ye took yesterday,
and the gold which thou didst promise, and I will go far
away from the city." Areobindus gave him the count Basil,
and the men whom they had taken from him, who were
fourteen in number, and made an agreement with him
to give him 2000 pounds of gold at [the end] of twelve
days. Ḳawâd struck his camp, and went and pitched at

---

* The village of Ḳubbê (perhaps identical with the ܒܝܬ ܩܘܒܐ, *Bibl.*

Orient., t. ii, p. 109, col. 2, i.e. دير القباب, for ܩܘܒܐ seems to be the

plural of קוּבְּתָא, القبّة) probably lay southeastwards from Edessa towards
Harrân, in which direction Ḳawâd retreated.

Dahbânâ *. He did not, however, wait till the appointed time (προθεσμία), but sent the very next day one of his men, named Hormizd, and ordered him to fetch three hundred pounds of gold. Areobindus summoned to him the grandees of the city, that they might consider how this money could be collected. When they saw that Hormizd had come in haste, they strengthened themselves in reliance on Christ, and took heart and said to Areobindus : "We will not send the money to this false man, because, just as he has gone back from his word, and has not waited till the day came which thou didst appoint for him, so will he go back and deceive when he has got the money. We believe that, if he fights with us, he will be again put to shame, because Christ stands in front of our city." Then Areobindus too took courage and sent to Ḳawâd, saying : "Now we know that thou art no king; for he is not a king who says a word and goes back (from it) and deceives. And if he deceives, he is no king. Therefore, as falsehood is manifest in thee, send me back the count Basil, and do thy worst."

LXII. Then Ḳawâd became furious, and armed the elephants which were with him, and set out, he and all his host, and came again to fight with Edessa, on the 24th of the month of Îlûl (September), a Wednesday. He surrounded the city on all sides, more than on the former occasion, all its gates being open. Areobindus ordered the Greek soldiers not to fight with him, that no falsehood might appear on his part; but some few of the villagers who were in the city went out against him with slings, and smote many of his mail-clad warriors, whilst of themselves not one fell. His legions (λεγεῶνες) were daring enough to try to enter the city; but when they came near its gates, like an upraised mound of earth †, they were humbled and repressed and turned back. Because, however, of the

---

* See Lebeau, *op. cit.*, t. iii, p. 65; t. vii, p. 367. The Arabs call it

الذَّهبانة or الذَّهبانيَّة. It lies nearly S. of Edessa, beyond Ḥarrân, on the road to ar-Raḳḳah.

† The comparison seems to be that of the compact mass of shieldbearing warriors in their charge to a moving mound of earth.

swiftness of the charge * of their cavalry, the slingers became mixed up among them; and though the Persians were shooting arrows, and the Huns were brandishing maces, and the Arabs were levelling spears at them, they were unable to harm a single one of them; but like those Philistines who went up against Samson, who, though they were many and armed, were unable to slay him, whilst he, though destitute of weapons, slew a thousand of them with the jaw-bone of an ass, so also the Persians and Huns and Arabs, though they and their horses were falling by the stones which the slingers were throwing, were unable to slay even a single one of them. After they saw that they were able neither to enter the city nor to harm the unarmed men who were mixed up with them, they set fire to the church of S. Sergius and the church of the Confessors and to all the convents that had been left (standing), and to the church of (the village of) Negbath, which the people of the city had spared.

LXIII. When the general (στρατηλάτης) Areobindus saw the zeal of the villagers, and that they were not put to shame, but that (the Divine) help went with them, he summoned all the villagers that were in Edessa next day to the (Great) Church, and gave them three hundred dînârs as a present. Ḳawâd departed from Edessa, and went and pitched on the river Euphrates; and thence he sent ambassadors to the emperor to inform him of his coming. The Arabs that were with him crossed the river westwards, and plundered and laid waste and took captive and burned everything in their way. Some few of the Persian cavalry went to Baṭnân (Batnae), and because its wall was broken down, they could not resist them, but admitted them without fighting and surrendered the town to them.

LXIV. *The year 815* (A.D. 503—4). When the Greek emperor learned what had happened, he sent his magister † Celer ‡ with a large army. When Ḳawâd heard this, he

---

* Literally "the letting go." In a glossary I find ܡܲܚܦܹܐ explained by ܡܚܒܨܦ݂ܐ ܒ̈ܛܠܩ, i.e., *divorce*.

† See the note on this word in ch. lix, at p. 50.

‡ Κελέριος, Κέλερ, or Κέλλωρ. See Lebeau, *op. cit.*, t. vii, p. 369.

directed his marches along the river Euphrates that he might
go and stay in that province of his which is called Bêth
Armâyê *. When he came nigh Callinîcus (ar-Raḳḳah), he
sent thither a general (*marzĕbân*) to fight with them. The dux
Timostratus came out against him, and destroyed his whole
army and took him alive. When Ḳawâd arrived at the city, he
drew up his whole force against it, threatening to rase it and
to put all its inhabitants to the sword or carry them off as
captives, if they did not give him up to him. The dux
was afraid of the vast host of the Persians, and gave him up.

LXV. When the magister Celerius arrived at Mabbôg,
which is on the river Euphrates †, and saw that Ḳawâd·had
moved away his camp before him, and moreover that the
winter season was come, and that he could not go after him, he
called the Greek generals, and rebuked them because they had
not hearkened one to another, and assigned them cities in which
to winter till the time for campaigning came·again.

LXVI. On the 25th of the first Kânûn (December) there
came an edict from the emperor that the tax (συντέλεια)
should be remitted to all Mesopotamia. The Persians who
were in Âmid, when they saw that the Greek army had gone
far away from them, opened the gates of the city of Âmid, and
went forth and entered where they pleased, and sold to the
merchants copper and iron and lead and old clothes and
whatever was to be had in it, and established in it a public
magazine (ἀπόθετον). When Patricius heard this, he set out
from Melitênê (Malaṭia), where he was wintering, and came and
pitched against Âmid. All the merchants whom he found
carrying down thither grain and oil, and those too who were
buying things from thence, he slew. He found also the
Persians who were sent by Ḳawâd to convey thither arms and
grain and cattle, and destroyed them, and took all that was with
them. When Ḳawâd learned this, he sent against him a

* "The land of the Arameans," the northern part of Babylonia, called by the
Arabs سَوَاد الكُوفَة or the cultivated district of al-Kûfah, in which lay Seleucia
and Ktêsiphôn, Kôchê and Mâhûzâ. See Noeldeke in the *Zeitschrift d. D. M. G.*,
Bd xxv, p. 113.

† This is not strictly correct. See Noeldeke in the *Zeitschrift d. D. M. G.*
Bd xxv, p. 351, note 2.

general (*marzĕbân*) to take vengeance on him. When they came near one another to fight, the Greeks, because of the fear inspired by their former defeat, counselled Patricius to flee, and he hearkened to this. In their haste, not knowing whither they were going, they came upon the river Kallath *; and because it was winter and there was a great flood in it, they were not able to cross it, but every one of them who hastened to cross was drowned in the river with his horse. When Patricius saw this, he exhorted the Greeks, saying : "O men of Greece, let us not put to shame our race and. our profession, and flee from our enemies, but let us turn against them, and perhaps we may be a match for them. And if they be too strong for us, it is better to die by the edge of the sword with a good name for valour than to perish like cowards by drowning." Then the Greeks listened to his advice, being constrained by the river; and they turned against the Persians with fury and destroyed them, and took their generals alive. Thereafter they again encamped against Âmid, and Patricius sent and collected unto him artisans from other cities and many of the villagers, and bade them dig in the ground and make a mine beneath the wall, that it might be weakened and fall.

LXVII. In the month of Âdar (March), when the rest of the Greeks were assembling to go down with the magister, a certain sign was given them from God, that they might be encouraged and be confident of victory. We were informed of this in writing by the people of the church of Zeugma †. That it may not be thought that I say anything on my own authority, or that I have hearkened to and believed a false rumour, I quote the very words of the letter that came to us, which are as follows.

---

* The name is pointed ܟܠܬ in the *Ecclesiastical History* of John of Ephesus, ed. Cureton, p. 416, 14, and ܟܠܬ in Knös, *Chrestomathia*, p. 79, 6. There can be no doubt that the *Kallath* is the Νυμφίος or Νυμφαῖος ποταμός (the Batman-sû), for ܐܩܒܣ (John of Ephesus, *loc. cit.*) is τὸ Ἀκβάς (Theophylact. Simocatta, *Historiae*, i. 12). Yet the distance seems very great; and, besides, one would rather have expected the Greeks to flee in a westerly or north westerly direction.

† Ζεῦγμα, on the Euphrates, near the modern Bir or Bîrejik.

LXVIII. "Hearken now to a marvel and a glorious sight, such as hath never been, because this concerns us and you and all the Greeks. For it is a wondrous thing, which it is hard for the understanding of men to believe. But we have seen it with our eyes, and touched it (with our hands), and read it with our lips. Ye ought therefore to believe it without any scruple. On the 19th of Âdâr (March), a Friday, which is the day that our Saviour was slain, a goose laid an egg in the village of 'Âgâr * in the district of Zeugma, and thereon were written Greek letters, fair and legible, which formed as it were the body of the egg and were raised to the sight and touch, like the letters which monks trace on the eucharistic cups †, so that even the blind could feel their shape. They were thus. A cross was traced on the side of the egg, and going completely round the egg, from it until it came to it again, was written THE GREEKS. And again there was traced another cross, and [going round the egg,] from it until it came to it again, was written SHALL CONQUER. The crosses were traced one above the other, and the words were written one above the other. There was none that saw this marvel, Christian or Jew, who restrained his mouth from uttering praise. But as for the letters which the right hand of God traced in the ovary (of the bird) ‡, we do not dare to imitate them, for they are very beautiful. Whosoever therefore hears it, let him believe it without hesitation." These are the words of the letter of the Zeugmatites §. As for the egg, those in whose village it was laid gave it to Areobindus.

LXIX. The Greeks collected a large army, and went down and encamped beside the city of Râs-'ain. By Ḳawâd too

---

* So Assemâni, *Bibl. Orient.*, t. i, p. 278, col. 2. The word is no longer clearly legible, and might be 'Âgâd. The vowels of course are doubtful

† Literally, "the cup of the blessing", supposing ‏ܩܣܘ̈ܪ̈ ܩܣܬ‎ to mean ποτήριον τῆς εὐλογίας = ποτήριον μυστικόν. Martin takes ‏ܩܣܬ‎, as he writes the word, to represent πιθάριον, meaning thereby, I suppose, πυξίον ἱερόν. This is quite compatible with the meaning of εὐλογία (see Du Cange); but is πιθάριον so used? It must be admitted that the word is not quite legible in the MS., and looks more like ‏ܩܣܬ‎ than anything else.

‡ Literally, "womb."

§ ‏ܙܘܓܡܛܝܐ‎ is formed from the Greek Ζευγματεύς or Ζευγματίτης. Compare ‏ܩܘܪܪܣܛܐ‎, Κυρρηστής or Κυρρέστης, from ‏ܩܘܪܘܣ‎, Κύρρος.

about 10,000 men were sent to go against Patricius. They took up their quarters in Nisîbis, that they might rest there, and they sent their cattle to pasture in the hills of Shîgâr. When the Magister heard this, he sent Timostratus, the dux of Callinîcus, with 6000 cavalry, and he went and fell upon those who were tending the horses and destroyed them, and carried off the horses and sheep and much booty, and returned to the Greek army at Râs-'ain. Then they all set out in a body, and went and encamped against the city of Âmid beside Patricius.

LXX. In the month of Îyâr (May) Calliopius the Aleppine became hyparch*. He came and settled at Edessa, and gave the Edessenes wheat to make bread for the soldiers (βουκελλάτον) at their own expense. They baked at this time 850,000 modii of wheat. Appion went to Alexandria, that he might make soldiers' bread there also and send a supply.

LXXI. As soon as Patricius had got under the wall of Âmid by means of the mine which he had dug, he propped it up with beams and set fire to them, whereby the outer face of the wall was loosened and fell down, but the inner part remained standing. He then thought of digging on by that mine and entering the city. When they had carried the excavation through, and the Greeks had begun to ascend, a woman of Âmid saw them and cried out suddenly for joy, "The Greeks are entering the city!" The Persians heard her, and ran at the first who came up and stabbed him. After him there came up a Goth, whose name was Ald †, who had been made tribune ‡ at Ḥarrân, and he stabbed three of those Persians. Not another one of the Greeks came up after him, because the Persians had perceived them. When Ald saw that no one was coming up, he became afraid and turned back; but he thought that he would take down with him the dead body of the Greek

---

* See p. 44, note ‡.

† I am not at all sure that I have called the Gothic warrior by his right name. The Syriac letters give us only *Ald*, *Eld* or *Ild*, which might be *Aldo*, *Haldo* (Förstemann, *Altdeutsches Namenbuch*, Bd i, col. 45); or *Helido*, *Allido* (ibid., col. 597); or *Hildi*, *Hildo* (ibid., col. 665). The well known name of *Alatheus*, *Alotheus*, or *Allothus* (ibid., col. 41), would probably have been spelled by our author with a soft *t*, viz. ܐܠܕ.

‡ Τριβοῦνος = χιλίαρχος. See Du Cange.

who had fallen, that the Persians might not insult it. As he was dragging away the dead body and going down into the mouth of the mine, the Persians smote him too and wounded him; and they directed thither the water from a large well that was near to it, and drowned four of the mail-clad Greeks who were about to come up. The rest fled and escaped thence. The Persians collected stones from within the city and blocked up the mine, and piled up a great quantity of earth over it, and all of them kept watch carefully round it, lest it should be excavated at some other spot. They dug ditches * within along the whole wall all round, and filled them with water, so that, if the Greeks should make another mine, the water might trickle into it, and it so become known. When Patricius heard this from a deserter who had come down to him, he gave up constructing mines.

LXXII. One day, when the whole Greek army was still and quiet, fighting was stirred up on this wise. A boy was feeding the camels and asses; and an ass, as it grazed, walked gradually close up to the wall. The boy was afraid to go in and fetch it; and one of the Persians, when he saw it, descended by a rope from the wall, and was going to cut it in pieces and carry it up to be food for them, for there was no meat at all inside the city. But one of the Greek soldiers, a Galilaean by race, drew his sword, and took his shield in his left hand, and ran at the Persian to kill him. As he had come close up to the wall, those who were standing on the wall threw down a large stone and crushed the Galilaean; and the Persian began to ascend to his place by the rope. When he had got halfway up the wall, one of the Greek officers drew nigh, with two shield-bearers walking before him, and shot an arrow from between them, and struck the Persian, and laid him beside the Galilaean. A shout went up from both sides, and because of this they became excited and rose up to fight. All the Greek troops surrounded the city in a dense mass, and there fell of them forty men, while one hundred and fifty were wounded. Of the Persians who were on the wall only nine were seen to be killed, and a few were wounded; for it was difficult to fight with them, the more so as they were on the top of the wall, because they had made for

* φόσσαι. See p. 41, note *.

themselves small houses all along the wall, and they were
standing within them and fighting, and could not be seen by
those who were without.

LXXIII. The Magister and the generals then thought that
it was not fitting for them to fight with them, because victory
did not depend for the Greeks upon the slaying of these,
seeing that they had to carry on war against the whole
of the Persians; and if Ḳawâd were to be defeated, these
would have to surrender or to perish in their prison. Therefore they gave orders that no one should fight with them,
lest by reason of those who were slain or wounded among
the Greeks, a great part of the army should disperse out of
fear.

LXXIV. In the month of Khazîrân (June), Constantine,
who had gone over to the Persians (see ch. xlviii), after he saw
that their cause did not prosper, fled from them, he and two
women of rank from Âmid, who had been given to him
(as wives) by the Persian king. For fourteen days he travelled
night and day through the uninhabited desert with a few
followers; and when he reached an inhabited spot, he made
himself known to the Greek Arabs, and they took him and
brought him to the fort * which is called Shûrâ †, and thence
they sent him to Edessa. When the emperor heard of his
arrival (there), he sent for him (to Constantinople); and when
he had come up to him, he ordered one of the bishops to
ordain him priest, and bade him go and dwell in the city of
Nicaea, and not come into his presence nor meddle with affairs
(of state).

LXXV. As Ḳawâd, when he took Âmid, had gone into its
public bath (δημόσιον) and experienced the benefit of bathing,

* The Latin word *castrum* remained appended to many Syrian names in the
form of ܩܣܛܪܐ or ܩܣܛܪܐ, (whence the Arabic قصر), like *caster, cester,
chester*, in our own country.

† When we last heard of this traitor, he was at Nisîbis (ch. lv). He probably
fled thence, and crossed the desert in a southwesterly direction till he approached
the Euphrates near Σοῦρα, or τὸ Σούρων πόλισμα, now *Sûriyeh*, above ar-Raḳḳah.
There seems to be no reason for believing him to have been shut up in Âmid,
as Lebeau thinks (*op. cit.*, t. vii, p. 372), following Assemâni (*Bibl. Orient.*, t. i,
p. 279, col. 1).

he gave orders, as soon as he went down to his own country, that baths (βαλανεῖα) should be built in all the towns of the Persian territory. 'Adîd* the Arab, who was under the rule of the Persians, surrendered with all his troops and became subject to the Greeks. Again, in the month of Tammûz (July), the Greeks fought with the Persians who were in Âmid, and Gainas †, the dux of Arabia ‡, smote many of them with arrows. When the day became hot, his armour got too warm for him, and he loosened the belt of his mail a little; whereupon they shot from Âmid arrows from the ballistae, and smote him, and he died. When the Magister saw that he suffered harm by sitting before Âmid, he took his army and went down to the Persian territory, leaving Patricius at Âmid. Areobindus too took his army and entered Persian Armenia; and they destroyed of the Armenians and Persians 10,000 men, and took captive 30,000 women and children, and plundered and burned many villages. When they came back to return to Âmid, they brought 120,000 sheep and oxen and horses. As they were passing by Nisîbis, the Greeks lay in ambush, and the few whose charge it was drove them past the city. When a certain general (marzĕbân) who was there saw that they were few in number, he armed his troops and sallied forth to take them from them. They pretended to flee, and the Persians took courage and pursued them. When they had gone a long way from their supports, the Greeks arose from the ambush and destroyed them, and not one of them escaped. They were about 7000 men. Mushlek (Mushegh) the Armenian, who was under the Persians, surrendered with his whole force and became subject to the Greeks.

LXXVI. *The year* 816 (A.D. 504—5). The fugitives and those who had escaped the sword, that were left in Âmid of its inhabitants, were in sore trouble and distress from famine. The Persians were afraid of them lest they should give up the

---

* The name is uncertain, but the MS. has ܐܕܝܕ, not ܐܕܝܕ, as Assemâni read, *Bibl. Orient.*, t. i, p. 279. This cannot be the successor to Na'mân, of whose appointment by Ḳawâd we were informed in ch. lviii, but only the shaikh of some tribe.

† ܓܐܝܣ. Probably Γαϊνᾶς or Γαινᾶς, rather than Γεννᾶῖος.

‡ Meaning the district around Damascus.

city to the Greeks; and they bound all the men that were
there, and threw them into the amphitheatre (κυνήγιον), and
there they perished of hunger and of endless bonds. But to
the women they gave part of their food, because they used them
to satisfy their lust, and because they had need of them to
grind and bake for them. When, however, food became scarce,
they neglected them, and left them without sustenance. For
none of them received more than one handful of barley daily
during this year; whilst of meat, or wine, or any other article of
food, they had absolutely none at all. And because they were
very much afraid of the Greeks, they never stirred from their
posts, but made for themselves small furnaces upon the wall,
and brought up handmills, and ground that handful of barley
where they were, and baked and ate it. They also brought up
large kneading-troughs, and placed them between the battlements, and filled them with earth, and sowed in them vegetables,
and whatever grew in them they ate.

LXXVII. In narrating what the women of the place did, I
may perhaps not be believed by those who come after us, (but)
at the present day there is no one of those who care to learn
things that has not heard all that was done, even though he be
at a great distance from us. Many women then met and
conspired together, and used to go forth by stealth into the
streets of the city in the evening or morning; and whomsoever
they met, woman or child or man, for whom they were a match,
they used to carry him by force into a house and kill and eat
him, either boiled or roasted. When this was betrayed by the
smell of the roasting, and the thing became known to the
general (marzĕbán) who was there (in command), he made an
example of many of them and put them to death, and told the
rest with threats that they should not do this again nor kill any
one. He gave them leave however to eat those that were dead,
and this they did openly, eating the flesh of dead men; and
the rest of them were picking up shoes and old soles and other
nasty things from the streets and courtyards, and eating them.
To the Greek troops however nought was lacking, but everything was supplied to them in its season, and came down with
great care by the order of the emperor. Indeed the things that
were sold in their camps were more abundant than in the cities,

whether meat or drink or shoes or clothing. All the cities were baking soldiers' bread (βουκελλάτον) by their bakers, and sending it to them, especially the Edessenes; for the citizens baked in their houses this year too. by order of Calliopius the hyparch, 630,000 modii, besides what the villagers baked throughout the whole district (χώρα), and the bakers, both strangers (ξένιοι) and natives.

LXXVIII. This year Mâr Peter the bishop went up again to the emperor to ask him to remit the tax (συντέλεια). The emperor answered him harshly, and rebuked him for having neglected the charge of the poor at a time like this and having come up to him (at Constantinople); for he said that God himself would have put it into his heart, if it had been right, without any one persuading him, to do a favour to the blessed city (of Edessa). Whilst the bishop was still there, however, the emperor sent the remission for all Mesopotamia by the hands of another, without his being aware of it. To the district of Mabbôg also he remitted one-third of the tax.

LXXIX. The Greek generals who were encamped by Âmid were going down on forays into the Persian territory, plundering and taking captive and destroying, and the Persians migrated before them, and crossed the Tigris. They found there the Persian cavalry, who were gathered together to come against the Greeks, and so they took heart against them, and halted on the farther bank of the Tigris. The Greeks crossed after them, and destroyed all the Persian cavalry, who were about 10,000 men, and plundered the property of all the fugitives. They burned many villages, and killed every male that was in them from twelve years old and upwards, but the women and children they took prisoners. For the Magister had thus commanded all the generals, that if any one of the Greeks was found saving a male from twelve years old and upwards, he should be put to death in his stead; and whatsoever village they entered, that they should not leave a single house standing in it. For this reason he set apart some stalwart men of the Greeks, and many villagers that accompanied them as they went down; and after the roofs were burned and the fire was gone out, they used to pull down the walls too. They also cut down and destroyed the vines and olives and all the trees.

The Greek Arabs too crossed the Tigris in front of them, and plundered and took captive and destroyed all that they found in the Persian territory. As I know thou studiest everything with great care, thy holiness must be well aware of this, that to the Arabs on both sides this war was a source of much profit, and they wrought their will upon both kingdoms.

LXXX. When Ḳawâd saw that the Greeks were ravaging the country, and that there was no one to oppose them, he wished to go and meet them. For this reason he sent an Astabîd* to the Magister to speak of peace, having with him an army of about 20,000 men. He sent all the men of note whom he had led captive from Âmid, and Peter, whom he had brought from Ashparîn (see ch. lvii), and Basil, whom he had taken from Edessa as a hostage (see ch. lxi). He sent also the dead body of the dux Olympius (see ch. li), who had gone down to him on an embassy and died, sealed up in a coffin (γλωσσόκομον), to show that he had not died by any other than a natural death, whereof his servants and those who came down with him were witnesses. The Magister received them, and sent them to Edessa, with the exception of the governor of Âmid and the count Peter; for he was very angry and provoked, and wanted to put them to death, saying that by their remissness the places which they guarded had been betrayed, and the Persians themselves testified that the wall of Âmid was impregnable. The Astabîd was begging and imploring of him to give him the Persians who were shut up in Âmid in place of those whom he had brought to him; because, though they were holding out from fear, yet they were in great distress through hunger. But the Magister said, " Do not mention the subject of these to me, because they are shut up in our city, and they are our slaves." The Astabîd says to him, " Well then, allow me to send them food, for it is unseemly for thee that thy slaves should die of hunger; for whenever thou pleasest, it is easy for thee to kill them." He says to him, " Send it." The Astabîd says, " Do thou swear unto me, and all thy generals and officers that are with thee, that no one shall kill those whom I send." They all

* See p. 50, note †.

took the oath, save the dux Nonnosus *, who was not with them by preconcerted arrangement, for the Magister had left him behind on purpose, so that, if there should be any oath taken, he might not be bound by it. The Astabîd therefore sent three hundred camels laden with sacks of bread, in the middle of which were placed arrows. Nonnosus fell upon them and took them from them, and slew those who were with them. When the Astabîd complained of this, and asked the Magister to punish the man who had done it, the Magister said to him, " I cannot find out who has done this, because of the great size of the army that is with me ; but if thou knowest who it is, and hast strength to take vengeance on him, I will not hinder thee." The Astabîd however was afraid to do this, and kept asking for peace.

LXXXI. When many days had passed after his asking (for peace), great cold set in, with much snow and ice, and the Greeks left their camps, one by one. Each man carried off what booty he had got, and set out to convey it to his own place. Those who remained and did not go to their homes, went into Tellâ and Râs-'ain and Edessa, to shelter themselves from the cold. When the Astabîd saw that the Greeks had become remiss and could not withstand the cold, he sent word to the Magister, saying, " Either make peace, and let the Persians go forth from Âmid, or accept war." The Magister commanded the count Justin to reassemble the army, but he was unable. When he saw that the greater part of the Greeks were dispersed and had left him, he made peace and let the Persians come out from Âmid on these terms, that, if the peace which they had concluded pleased the two soverains (Anastasius and Ḳawâd), and they set their seal to what they had done, (it should stand) ; but if not, the war should go on between them. When the Greek emperor learned these things, he gave orders that a public magazine (ἀπόθετον) should be established in every city, but especially at Âmid, with the view of putting an

---

* The manuscript appears to have ‎‎⟨Syriac⟩, and not, as Martin has given, ‎⟨Syriac⟩. This latter is certainly not a common form of the name *John*, and our author elsewhere uses ‎⟨Syriac⟩. I have followed Assemâni in representing ‎⟨Syriac⟩ by Νόννοσος, but it might possibly be Νόννειος or Νώνιος, Nonius.

end to hostility and drawing closer the bonds of peace. He also sent gifts and presents to Ḳawâd by the hand of a man named Leôn, and a service for his table, all the pieces of which were of gold.

LXXXII. How much the Edessenes suffered, who conveyed corn down to Âmid, no man knows but those who were actually engaged in the work; for the greater part of them died by the way, themselves and their cattle.

LXXXIII. The excellent John, bishop of Âmid *, went to his rest before the Persians laid siege to it; and its clergy (κλῆρος) went up to the holy and God-loving, the adorned with all divine beauties, the strenuous and illustrious Mâr Flavian †, patriarch (πατριάρχης) of Antioch, to ask him to appoint a bishop for them. He treated them with great honour during the whole time that they stayed there. Afterwards, when the excellent Nonnus, priest and steward of the church of Âmid, escaped from captivity, the clergy (κληρικοί) asked the patriarch and he made him their bishop ‡. When the excellent Nonnus had been ordained bishop, he sent his suffragan (χωρεπίσκοπος) Thomas to Constantinople, to fetch the Âmidenes who were there and to ask a donation from the emperor. Those who were there conspired with him, and asked the emperor that Thomas himself might be their bishop. The emperor granted their prayer, and sent word to the patriarch not to constrain them. The emperor also gave them the governor whom they asked for. The emperor and the patriarch gave presents to the church of Âmid, and a large sum of money to be distributed among the poor. For this reason there flocked thither all those who were wandering about in other places, and they were carrying forth the corpses of the dead every day out of Âmid, and were then receiving what was appointed for them.

LXXXIV. Urbicius (Οὐρβίκιος), the emperor's minister, who had bestowed large gifts in the district of Jerusalem and in other places, went down thither also, and gave there a dînâr a piece (to the inhabitants). He returned thence to Edessa, where he gave to every woman who chose to take it a

---

* See Le Quien, *Oriens Christ.*, t. ii, col. 992.

† Flavian II. See Le Quien, *loc. cit.*, col. 729.

‡ See Le Quien, *loc. cit.*, col. 992.

trimêsion *, and to every child a dirham (*zûzâ*). Nearly all the women took it, both those that were needy and those that were not.

LXXXV. In this same year, after the fighting had ceased, the wild beasts became very ferocious against us. In consequence of the great number of dead bodies of those who had fallen in these battles, they had acquired a taste for eating human flesh; and when the bodies of the slain rotted and disappeared, the wild beasts entered the villages and carried off children and devoured them. They also fell upon single men on the roads and killed them. At last they became so afraid that, at the time of threshing, not a man in the whole district would pass the night in his threshingfloor without a hut (to shelter him), for fear of the beasts of prey. But by the help of our Lord, who is always careful for us and delivers us from all trials by His mercy, some of them fell by the hands of the villagers, who stabbed them, and sent their dead carcases to Edessa; and others were caught by huntsmen, who bound them and brought them (thither) alive, so that every one saw them and praised God, who has said †, "The fear of you and the dread of you I will put upon every beast of the earth." For although, because of our sins, war and famine and pestilence and captivity and noxious beasts and other chastisements, written and unwritten, were sent upon us, yet by His grace we have been delivered from them all.

LXXXVI. Me too, a feeble man, He hath strengthened because of His mercy, through thy prayers, that I should write to the best of my ability some of the things that have happened, as a reminder to those who endured them, and for the instruction of those who shall come after us, that, if they please, they may be enabled to become wise through these few things which I have written. For the things that I have omitted are far more than those which I have recorded; and indeed I said from the beginning that I was not able to recount them all; because the sufferings which each individual alone endured, if they were written down, would form long narratives, for which a big book would not suffice. And thou must know from what

* Τριμήσιον, τριμίσιον, *tremissis*, the third of an *aureus*.
† Genesis, ch. ix. 2.

others have written, that those too who came to our aid under
the name of deliverers, both when going down and when coming
up, plundered us almost as much as enemies *. Many poor
people they turned out of their beds and slept in them, whilst
their owners lay on the ground in cold weather. Others they
drove out of their own houses, and went in and dwelt in them.
The cattle of some they carried off by force as if it were spoil of
war; the clothes of others they stripped off their persons and
took away. Some they beat violently for a mere trifle; with
others they quarrelled in the streets and reviled them for a
small cause. They openly plundered every one's little stock
of provisions, and the stores that some had laid up in the
villages and cities. Many they fell upon in the highways.
Because the houses and inns of the city (of Edessa) were not
sufficient for them, they lodged with the artisans in their shops.
Before the eyes of every one they illused the women in the
streets and houses. From old women, widows and poor, they
took oil, wood, salt, and other things, for their own expenses;
and they kept them from their own work to wait upon them.
In short, they harassed every one, both great and small, and
there was not a person left who did not suffer some harm from
them. Even the nobles of the land, who were set to keep them
in order and to give them their billets, stretched out their hands
for bribes; and as they took them from every one, they spared
nobody, but after a few days sent other soldiers to those upon
whom they had quartered them in the first instance. They
were billeted even upon the priests and deacons, though these
had a letter (σάκρα) from the emperor exempting them there-
from. But why need I weary myself in setting forth many
things, which even those who are greater than I are unable to
recount ?

LXXXVII. After he had recrossed the river Euphrates
westwards, the Magister went to the emperor (at Constantinople);
and Areobindus went to Antioch, Patricius to Melitênê
(Malaṭia), Pharazmân to Apameia (Fâmiyah), Theodore to
Darmĕsûk (Damascus), and Calliopius to Mabbôg (Menbij).
So there was a little breathing-space at Edessa, and the few

* The description of the Gothic mercenaries in this and the following chapters
is not without its peculiar interest and value.

people that remained in it were glad. Eulogius the governor was busying himself in rebuilding the town; and the emperor [gave him] two hundred pounds (of gold) for the expenses of the building. He rebuilt and restored the [whole] outer wall that goes round the city. He also restored and repaired the two aqueducts (ἀγωγοί) that come in from the village of Tell-Zĕmâ and from Maudad *; and rebuilt and finished the public bath that fell down (see ch. xxx). He likewise repaired his own palace (πραιτώριον), and built a great deal throughout the whole city. The emperor too gave the bishop twenty pounds (of gold) for the expenses of repairing the wall; and the minister Urbicius gave him ten pounds to build a church to the blessed Mary. But the oil which had been supplied to the churches and convents from the public oilstore, amounting to 6800 ḳesṭê † (per annum), the governor took away from them, and ordered it to be used for burning in the porticoes of the city. The vergers (παραμονάριοι) besought him much regarding it, but he would not listen to them. That he might not be thought, however, to despise the churches built for God, he gave of his own property to every church two hundred ḳesṭê. Up to this year wheat had been sold at the rate of four modii for a dînâr, and barley six modii, and wine two measures; but after the new harvest wheat was sold at the rate of six modii for a dînâr, and barley ten modii.

LXXXVIII. The Persian Arabs were never at peace or rest, but they crossed over into the Greek territory, without the Persians, and took captive (the people of) two villages. When the general (marzĕbân) of the Persians, who was at Nisîbis, learned this, he took their shaikhs and put them to

---

* Both these villages evidently lay to the N. of Edessa. The Germish-Chai rises, two or three hours' journey from the city, near a place called Burac or Berik, a little south of which are the remains of the arches of an ancient aqueduct, which entered Edessa on the north side, somewhere near the Gate of Beth-Shĕmesh. In the neighbourhood of Burac, therefore, Professor G. Hoffmann places Maudad (Modad) and Tell-Zĕmâ; though for the latter another locality may, he thinks, be possibly found. In the valley of the Râs-al-'ain Chai, near a place called Jurbân, Julbân, or Julmân, the ruins of another ancient aqueduct have been seen, and in this neighbourhood, a little way south of Dagouly or Tagula, Pococke mentions a place named Zoumey, which may perhaps be identical with Tell-Zĕmâ.

† Say quarts.

death. The Greek Arabs too crossed over without orders into
the Persian territory, and took captive (the people of) a hamlet.
When the Magister heard this, for he had gone down at the end
of this year to Apameia, he sent (orders) to Timostratus, the dux
of Callinîcus, and he seized five of their shaikhs, two of whom he
slew with the sword and impaled the other three. Pharazmân
set out from Apameia after the Magister had gone down
thither, and came and stayed at Edessa, and he received
authority from the emperor to become general in place of
Hypatius.

LXXXIX. The wall of Baṭnân-ḳaṣṭrâ *, in Sĕrûg, which
was all out of repair and breached, was rebuilt and renovated
by the care of Eulogius, the governor of Edessa. The excellent
priest Aedesius plated with copper the doors of the men's aisle
in the (Great) Church of Edessa.

XC. *The year* 817 (A.D. 505—6). The generals of the
Greek army informed the emperor that the troops suffered great
harm from their not having any (fortified) town situated on the
border. For whenever the Greeks went forth from Tellâ or
Âmid to go about on expeditions among the Arabs, they were
in constant fear, whenever they halted, of the treachery of
enemies; and if it happened that they fell in with a larger force
than their own, and thought of turning back, they had to endure
great fatigue, because there was no town near them in which
they could find shelter. For this reason the emperor gave
orders that a wall should be built for the village of Dârâ, which
is situated on the frontier. They selected workmen from all
Syria (for this task), and they went down thither and were
building it; and the Persians were sallying forth from Nisîbis
and forcing them to stop. On this account Pharazmân set
out from Edessa, and went down and dwelt at Âmid, whence
he used to go forth to those who were building and to give
them aid †. He also used to make great hunts after the wild
beasts, especially the wild boars, which had become numerous
there after the country was laid waste. He used to catch
more than forty of these in one day; and as a proof of his
skill he even sent some of them to Edessa, both alive and
dead.

* See p. 60, note *.   † See the note on the Syriac text.

XCI. The excellent Sergius*, bishop of Bîrtâ-ḳasṭra†, which is situated beside us on the river Euphrates, began likewise to build a wall to his town; and the emperor gave him no small sum of money for his expenses. The Magister also gave orders that a wall should be built to Eurôpus‡, which is situated to the west of the River in the prefecture (ἐπαρχία) of Mabbôg; and the people of the place worked at it as best they could.

XCII. After Pharazmân went down to Âmid, the dux Romanus came in his place, and settled at Edessa with his troops, and bestowed large alms upon the poor. The emperor added in this year to all his former good deeds, and sent a remission of the tax to the whole of Mesopotamia, whereat all the landed proprietors rejoiced and praised the emperor.

XCIII. But the common people were murmuring, and crying out and saying, "The Goths ought not to be billeted upon us, but upon the landed proprietors, because they have been benefited by this remission." The prefect (ὕπαρχος) gave orders that their request should be granted. When this began to be done, all the grandees of the city assembled unto the dux Romanus and asked of him, saying, "Let your highness give orders what each of these Goths should receive by the month, lest, when they enter the houses of wealthy people, they plunder them as they have plundered the common people." He granted their request, and ordered that they should receive an *espâda* § of oil per month, and two hundred pounds of wood, and a bed and bedding between each two of them.

* See Le Quien, *Oriens Christ.*, t. ii, col. 987.

† The expression "situated *beside us* on the river Euphrates" seems to make it almost certain that this Bîrtâ-ḳasṭrâ is identical with the modern Bîr or Bîrejiḳ. Compare ch. lxiii.

‡ Εὐρωπός or Ὠρωπός, ܐܘܪܘܦܘܣ, جِرْبَاس, or in the Arabic plural جِرَابِيس, *Jerâbis* (*Jerabolus* is a blunder of Maundrell's). See Hoffmann, *Auszüge aus syrischen Akten persischer Märtyrer* in the *Abhandlungen für d. Kunde d. Morgenlandes*, Bd vii, 3, p. 161.

§ Neither the exact form nor meaning of this word is quite certain, for besides ܐܣܦܕܐ we find ܐܣܦܕܐ and ܐܣܦܕܐ in the native dictionaries (see Payne Smith's *Thesaurus*). In Hoffmann's *Bar 'Ali*, no. 1031, it is explained to mean "a leaden vessel in which one cools wine or water, also called ܩܣܛܠܐ;

XCIV. When the Goths heard this order, they ran to attack the dux Romanus in the house of the family of Barsâ * and to kill him. As they were ascending the stairs of his lodging, he heard the sound of their tumult and uproar, and perceived what they wanted to do. He quickly put on his armour, and took up his weapons, and drew his sword, and stood at the upper door of the house in which he lodged. He did not however kill any one of the Goths, but (merely) kept brandishing his sword and hindering the first that came up from forcing their way in upon him. Those who were below were in their anger compelling those who were above them to ascend and force their way in upon him. Thus a great many people occupied the stairs of the house, as thy holiness well knoweth. When therefore the first who had gone up were unable to get in, because of their fear of the sword, and those behind were pressing upon them, many men occupied the stairs; and because of the weight they broke and fell upon them. A few of them were killed, but many had their limbs broken and were maimed, so that they could not be cured again. When Romanus had found an opportunity because of this accident, he fled upon the roof from one house to another and made his escape; but he said nothing more to them, and for this reason they remained where they were billeted, behaving exactly as they pleased, for there was none to check them or restrain or admonish them.

XCV. Our bishop Mâr Peter was very dangerously ill all this year. In the month of Nîsân (April) the distress became again much greater in our city; for the Magister collected his whole army, and arose to go down to the Persian territory to make and renew with them a treaty of peace. When he entered Edessa, ambassadors from the Persians came to him and informed him that the Aṣṭabîd who had come to meet him and conclude a peace with him was dead; and they begged of him and said that, if he came down for peace, he

---

a رَصَاصِيَّة or leaden vessel with a wide top." Martin gives from a Paris MS.,

زِيتِ نَيَلَ دِمَسِدا أَهُصَّرُ, i.e., "two φιάλαι of olive oil."

* There was a bishop of Edessa of this name. See Assemâni, *Bibl. Orient.*, t. i, pp. 396 and 398.

ought not to go beyond Edessa until another Astabîd should be
sent by the Persian king. He granted their request and stayed
at Edessa for five months. And because the city was not
·sufficient for the Goths who were with him, they were quartered
also in the villages, and likewise in all the convents, large and
small, that were around the city. Not even those who lived in
solitude were allowed to dwell in the quiet which they loved,
because upon them too they were quartered in their convents.

XCVI. Because they did not live at their own expense
from the very first day they came, they became so gluttonous in
their eating and drinking, that some of them, who had regaled
themselves on the tops of the houses, went forth by night, quite
stupefied with too much wine, and stepped out into empty
space, and fell headlong down, and so departed this life by an
evil end. Others, as they were sitting and drinking, sank into
slumber, and fell from the housetops, and died on the spot.
Others again suffered agonies on their beds from eating too
much. Some poured boiling water into the ears of those who
waited upon them for trifling faults. Others went into a
garden to take vegetables, and when the gardener arose to
prevent them from taking them, they slew him with an arrow,
and his blood was not avenged. Others still, as their wickedness increased and there was no one to check them, since those
on whom they were quartered behaved with great discretion and
did everything exactly as they wished, because they gave them
no opportunity for doing them harm, were overcome by their
own rage and slew one another. That there were among them
others who lived decently is not concealed from thy knowledge;
for it is impossible that in a large army like this there should
not be some such persons found. The wickedness of the bad,
however, went so far in evildoing that those too who were
illdisposed among the Edessenes dared to do something un-
seemly; for they wrote down on sheets of paper ($\chi\acute{a}\rho\tau\eta\varsigma$)
complaints against the Magister, and fastened them up secretly
in the customary places of the city (for public notices). When
he heard this, he was not angered, as he well might have been,
neither did he make any search after those who had done this,
nor think of doing any harm to the city, because of his good
nature; but he used all the diligence possible to quit Edessa
with haste and speed.

XCVII. *The year* 818 (A.D. 506—7) *. The Magister
therefore took his whole army, and went down to the border.
And there came to him a Persian ambassador to the town of
Dârâ, bringing with him hostages, who had been sent by the
Aṣṭabîd; and they also asked him, saying that, if he wished to
make peace, he too ought to send hostages (ὅμηροι) in place of
those whom he had received, and afterwards both parties would
draw nigh to one another in friendship, and they would meet
one another with five hundred horsemen apiece unarmed, and
then they would sit in council, and would do what was fitting.
He agreed to do what they asked, and sent hostages, and went
unarmed to meet the Aṣṭabîd on the day appointed. But
because he was afraid lest the Persians should commit some
treachery against him, he drew up the whole Greek army
opposite them under arms, and gave them a sign, and ordered
them, if they saw that sign, to come to him quickly. When
the Aṣṭabîd too was come to meet him, and the Greeks and all
the generals who were with them had seated themselves in
council, one of the Greek soldiers gave good heed and perceived
that all those who had come with the Aṣṭabîd wore armour
under their clothes. He made this known to the general
Pharazmân and the dux Timostratus, and they displayed that
signal to the troops, whereupon they at once set up a shout and
came to them, and took prisoners the Aṣṭabîd and those who
were with him among them. The troops that were in the
Persian camp, when they learned that the Aṣṭabîd and his
companions were taken prisoners, fled for fear of them, and
entered Nisîbis. The Greeks wished to take the Aṣṭabîd and
to kill those who were with him; but the Magister begged them
not to give an occasion for war and to drive away (all hopes of)
peace. With difficulty did they consent, but at last they
hearkened to him, and let the Aṣṭabîd and his companions
depart from among them, without having done them any hurt;
for even when victorious, the Greek generals were gentle.
When the Aṣṭabîd went to his camp, and saw that the Persians
had retired into Nisîbis, he was afraid to remain alone, and
went in also to join them. He tried to force them to go out
of the city with him, but they were unwilling to go out for fear.

* In the MS. there is a marginal note, no longer distinctly legible: "In this
year died the holy Mâr Shîlâ (Silas) of the village of B......."

In order that their fear might not become evident to the Greeks, the Aṣṭabîd sent and fetched his daughter to Nisîbis, and according to Persian custom took her to wife. When the Magister sent him a message to say, "No man will harm thee, even if thou comest forth alone", he returned for answer, "It is not out of fear that I do not go forth, but in order that the days of the wedding-feast may be fulfilled." Although the Magister knew the whole thing quite well, he passed it over just as if he did not.

XCVIII. And some days after, when the Aṣṭabîd came out to him, he gave up, for love of peace, all the things which he had determined to require of the Persians, and made a covenant with them, and concluded peace. They drew up documents between them, and appointed a fixed time, during which they were not to make war with one another; and all the armies were glad and rejoiced in the peace that was made.

XCIX. While they were still there on the frontier, Celerius the magister and Calliopius received a letter from the emperor Anastasius, which was full of care and compassion for the whole region of Mesopotamia; and thus he wrote to them, that, if they thought that the tax ($\sigma\nu\nu\tau\epsilon\lambda\epsilon\iota a$) ought to be remitted, they had full power to remit it without delay. They decided that the whole tax should be remitted to the district of Âmid, and the half of it to that of Edessa, and they sent and made this known in Edessa. And after a little while they sent another letter with the news of the peace.

C. On the 28th of the month of the latter Teshrî (November A.D. 506), he took his whole army and came up from the border. When he arrived at Edessa, the Magister had a mind not to enter it, because of their murmuring against him (see ch. xcvi). But the blessed Bar-hadad, bishop of Tellâ*, begged him not to allow resentment to get the better of him, nor to leave behind the feeling of vexation or annoyance in any one's mind. He readily acceded to his request; and all the Edessenes too came forth with much alacrity to meet him, carrying wax tapers ($\kappa\eta\rho\iota\omega\nu\epsilon s$), both young and old. All the clergy ($\kappa\lambda\eta\rho\iota\kappa o\iota$) likewise, and the members of religious orders, and the monks, came out with them; and they entered the city with great rejoicing. He sent on all his troops the very same day to con-

* See p. 48, note *.

tinue their march; but he himself remained for three days, and gave the governor two hundred dînârs to distribute in presents. And the people of the city, rejoicing in the peace that was made, and exulting in the immunity which they would henceforth enjoy from the distress in which they now were, and dancing for joy at the hope of the good things which they expected to arrive, and lauding God, who in His goodness and mercy had cast peace over the two kingdoms, escorted him as he set forth with songs of praise that befitted him and him who had sent him*.

CI. *If this emperor appears in a different aspect towards the end of his life, let no one be offended at his praises, but let him remember the things that Solomon did at the close of his life†.* These few things out of many I have written to the best of my ability unto thy charity, unwillingly and yet willingly. Unwillingly, on the one hand, in order that I might not weary the wise friend who knows these things better than I do. Willingly, on the other hand, for the sake of obeying thy command. Now therefore I beg of thee that thou too wouldest fulfil the promise contained in thy letter (see ch. i) to offer up prayer constantly on behalf of me a sinner. For now that I have learned thy wish, it shall be my greatest care, and whatever happens in the times that are coming and is worthy of record, I will write it down and send it to thee my father, if I remain alive. Let us therefore pray from this place, and thou my father from yonder, and all the children of men everywhere, that history may speak of the great change that is going to take place in the world; and just as we have been unable to describe the wants of these evil times as they really were, because of the abundance of their afflictions, so also may we be unable to tell of those that are coming, because of the multitude of their blessings. And may our words be too feeble to speak of the happy life of our fellow-citizens, and of the calm and peace that shall reign throughout the world, and of the great plenty that there shall be, and of the superabundance of the harvest of the blessing of God, who hath said ‡, "The former troubles shall be forgotten and shall be hidden from before us." To Him be glory for ever and ever, Amen.

---

* That befitted Celer and his master the emperor.

† This sentence is no doubt a later addition, probably from the pen of Dionysius of Tell-Maḥrê.   ‡ Isaiah, ch. lxv. 16.

INDEX.

of Âmid and the count Peter with death, 64; conference with the Aṣṭabîd regarding the Persian garrison of Âmid, *ib.*; refuses to punish Nonnosus, 65; concludes a provisional treaty with the Persians, 65; returns to the emperor, 68; returns to Apameia, 70; chastises the Greek Arabs, *ib.*; fortifies Eurôpus, 71; goes down to the Persian frontier to make peace, 72; complaints against him by the Edessenes, 73; quits Edessa, *ib.*; interview with the Aṣṭabîd, whom he takes prisoner, 74; concludes peace with the Persians and remits the taxes, 75; his return to and departure from Edessa, 75, 76.

Christ, our Lord Jesus, His promise to Abgâr regarding the city of Edessa, 5, 26, 51, 52.

Chrysargyron, remission of the, by Anastasius, 22.

Church of Arsamosata, destroyed by an earthquake, 25.

Church of the Apostles, at Edessa, 33.

Church of the Confessors, at Edessa, 51, 54.

Church of SS. Cosmas and Damianus, at Edessa, 51.

Church, the Great, at Edessa, 22, 32, 33, 70.

Church of S. John the Baptist and S. Addai, at Edessa, 20.

Church of Mâr Ḳônâ, at Edessa, 33.

Church of S. Mary the Virgin, to be built at Edessa, 69.

Church of SS. Sergius and Simeon, at Edessa, 22, 50, 51, 54.

Church of S. Thomas, at Edessa, 22, note ‖.

Comet seen at Edessa, A.D. 499, 27.

Constantina. See Tellâ.

Constantine the emperor, statue of, at Edessa, 19.

Constantine, governor of Theodosiûpolis, the traitor, 37; commands a Persian army, 44; deserts the Persians, 60; his treatment by the emperor, *ib.*

Cyrus, bishop of Edessa, 19; dies, 23.

Dahbânâ, 53.

Daiṣân, the river, 18.

Damascus, 68.

Dârâ, 44; fortified by the Greeks, 70.

Darmĕsûḳ, 68.

Demosthenes, appointed governor of Edessa, 23; goes on a visit to Constantinople, 30; returns to Edessa, 31; his care for the poor, 31, 32.

Earthquakes, 23—26, 37.

Edessa, impregnable, according to our Lord's promise, 5, 51, 52; refuses to admit Matronianus and his troops, 11; celebration of

Hypatius, a Greek general, besieges Âmid, 44, 45; replaced by Pharazmân, 70.

Illus, governor of Antioch, 9; Zênôn's attempt on his life at Constantinople, *ib.*; retires to Antioch, 10; rebels with Leontius against Zênôn, *ib.*; they conclude a treaty with the Persians, 11; quit Antioch, *ib.*; are defeated by John the Scythian, *ib.*; flee to the fortress of Papûrion, *ib.*; are taken and put to death, 12.

Isaurians, the, rebel against Anastasius, but are put down, 15.

Jacob of Batnae, his letters to the cities of Mesopotamia, 43.

Jerâbîs. See Eurôpus.

Jerusalem, 66.

Jews, treachery of the, at Tellâ, 47; they are massacred, 48.

John, bishop of Âmid, 66.

John the Scythian, sent against Illus and Leontius, 11; defeats them, *ib.*; besieges and takes Papûrion, 11, 12.

Jovinian, or Jovian, the Greek emperor, 7.

Julian, the Greek emperor, death of, 7.

Justin, the count, afterwards emperor, 65.

Ḳadishâyê, the, rebel against Ḳawâd, 14; besiege Nisîbis, *ib.*; submit to Ḳawâd, 16; join the Persian army, 46.

Ḳallath, the river, 56.

Ḳara Ḳoyûn, the. See Daiṣân.

Ḳawâd, king of Persia, is left as a hostage with the Huns by his father Pêrôz, 8; becomes king, 13; sends an embassy to Zênôn, *ib.*; favours the Zarâdushtaḳân, or Mazdakites, *ib.*; is hated by the Persian nobles, 14; who conspire against him, 15; flees to the Huns, *ib.*; marries his sister's daughter, *ib.*; returns to Persia with a Hunnish army and slays the nobles, 16; invades the Greek territory, *ib.*; reconquers the Armenians, *ib.*; invades Armenia, and takes Theodosiûpolis, 37; besieges Âmid, 38 sqq.; takes the town, 42; intends to besiege Edessa, 46; nominates a successor to Na'mân, 47; lays siege to Tellâ, 47; raises the siege, and marches against Edessa, 48; besieges Edessa, 51; retreats, 52; returns, 53; retreats again, 54; advances to the Euphrates, *ib.*; retires to Bêth-Armâyê, 55; sends troops against Patricius, 56, 57; builds baths in the Persian towns, 60, 61; sends an embassy to the magister Celer, 64.

Kĕphar Ṣĕlem. See Negbath.

Ḳônâ, bishop of Edessa, 33.

Ḳubbê, a village near Edessa, 52.

J. S.   *l*

ܡܟܬܒܢܘܬܐ ܕܬܫܥܝܬܐ ܕܙܒܢܐ[1] ܕܐܘܠܨܢܐ

ܕܗܘܐ ܒܐܘܪܗܝ ܘܒܐܡܝܕ ܘܒܟܠܗ̇[2] ܒܝܬ ܢܗܪܝܢ ܀

I. ܦܩܕܬ ܠܡܚܝܠܘܬܐ ܕܚܣܝܘܬܟ ܪܚܡܬ ܠܐܠܗܐ: ܐܘ ܡܝܬܪܐ ܕܒܢ̈ܝܢܫܐ ܘܟܗܢܐ ܘܪܝܫ ܕܝܪܐ ܣܪܓܝܣ: ܗܠܝܢ ܕܗܘܝ ܟܬܒܬ ܠܟ ܕܐܟܬܘܒ ܠܟ ܐܝܟ ܕܠܥܗܕܢܐ[3]: ܕܐܡܬܝ ܐܬܐ ܩܡܨܐ: ܘܐܡܬܝ ܟܦܢܐ ܣܓܝ[4]܆ ܘܐܡܬܝ ܗܘܐ ܫܚܢܐ ܘܟܘܪܗܢܐ ܘܡܟܬܫܢܘܬܐ܆

5 ܘܩܪܒܐ ܕܪ̈ܘܗܡܝܐ ܘܦܪ̈ܣܝܐ[5]. ܟܠ ܗܠܝܢ ܕܝܢ ܐܦ ܡܫ̈ܠܡܐ ܪܘ̈ܚܐ ܕܟܠܗ ܡܚܝܢܝܢ[6] ܗܘܘ ܒܗܝܢ. ܐܝܟ ܕܒܡܚܙܝܐ ܪܒܐ ܐܬܡܠܝܢ ܒܗ ܠܟ ܘܠܢܗܘܢ: ܟܕ ܕܐܦܠܐ ܚܕ ܡܢܗܘܢ ܡܚܝܢ ܠܗܘܢ ܒܚܒܠܐ. ܝܕܥ ܕܝܢ ܐܢܐ ܕܐܟܬܘܒ ܐܢܝܢ ܕܟܝ܆ ܘܠܐ ܣܦܩܬ ܚܝܠܐ ܕܬܢܝܬܐ܆ ܠܡܬܥܣܩܘ ܘܠܡܟܬܒܗ ܐܝܟ

---

1) Assemâni, *Bibl. Orient.*, t. i, p. 260, has ܕܙܒ̈ܢܐ, but it is very uncertain whether the points are really there. 2) MS. ܘܒܟܠܗ. 3) MS. ܕܠܥܗܕܢܐ. 4) MS. ܣܓܝ. 5) Assemâni, *op. cit.*, p. 261, has ܘܩܪܒܐ ܕܪ̈ܘܗܡܝܐ ܘܦܪ̈ܣܝܐ. 6) MS. ܡܚܝܢܝܢ (*sic*), but corrected on the margin.

II.

---

1) For . 2) The appears to be a later addition.
3) MS. (*sic*). 4) The is a later addition. 5) MS.
, but the seems to have been added here, as in many other
cases, by a later hand, and is in this instance incorrect, the fem.
 being required. 6) Read ‖. 7) MS. .
Martin read . 8) For . 9) Originally .
10) For .

III.
---

1) is on the margin.   2) MS. .   3) MS. apparently ; Martin, .   4) For .
5) MS. for .

---

1) For .   2) Martin read .   3) For
.   4) The is a later addition.   5) is wanting
in the MS. The in is more recent.   6) Read ؟
7) MS. .

IV.

5

10

15

20

---

1) MS. ܐܠܗܘܬܝ.   2) MS. ܐܘܢ.   3) The ܡ has in each case been subsequently scored out.   4) Read ܢܩܒܠ.

V.
---

1) The MS. appears to have , though the reading is no longer clear. 2) MS. . 3) MS. , wrongly, for the sense requires . 4) MS. . 5) MS. , which we might read . 6) MS. (sic).
7) MS. .

 VI.
---

1) MS. .   2) MS. .   3) MS. .
4) This passage is quoted by Assemâni, *Bibl. Orient.*, t. i, p. 261.
5) MS. , wrongly.   6) Read ?

VII.
1) Read ؟ 2) MS. . 3) MS. .
4) MS. apparently . 5) The ordinary way of spelling
this name is seems to be actually the read-
ing of the MS.; but I should prefer Martin's suggestion of
(which is really the reading of the MS. in ch. xlviii, ,) or else
Nöldeke's of .

VIII.

15 IX.
---

1) o is in both these cases a later addition.   2) We should probably read or . See Noeldeke, *Geschichte der Perser und Araber zur Zeit der Sasaniden*, p. 17, note 5; 99, note 1; 115, note 2.   3) Martin gives , which cannot be right. The word is no longer to be seen in the MS.   4) Here too o is a later addition.

 Lo
X. Loo 5
Lo Loo 10
 Loo
 Lo.

XI. 20
. Lo

<hr>

1) The last letters of this name are illegible in the MS.
2) This seems to be the reading of the MS. rather than .
3) MS. .   4) The MS. may perhaps have , or
, but it is doubtful.

XII.

20   XIII.

---

15 XIV.
---

1) See the same form in ch. lix.   2) MS. .   3) MS.
originally , but corrected.   4) MS. .   5) This
appears to be the reading of the MS., though is not quite certain.

ه‍، حكاٮٮٮٮٚا كٯٯحكٮ اک ٮجٟكحٯٯحٮٮ. ٯۿ ٱۻٱ ٯٯ ٮٯۺا
كٱٮٛمحٮصٮا ٱٮۦٮۿۯا٘ ٮۯۻا ٯٮ ٮكٯۿ. ٯۑۻٮا كٮ ٭حٮٮ كٯٯٮٮٮ
ٮۿ‍ۿٮا ٮٱٛٮٮٮٮٮ كٮ. ٮكٯۿ ٮٮٮ ٮ‍ٮ ٮٱٮ ٮٮٱٛ ٭حٮٮٮ حكٮۯ
ۿۯٮۺا؞ ٮٮٮٮ ٱٮ ٮٮ ٮٮٮٮٱ ۿٮٮٮكٱٮ ٮٱٮ ۻٱۻٮۯۿٯۦٮۦٛ؞

5 ٮحكۻكحٮٮ ٮۻٱ ٱٯٯٱ ٱٮٮٮ ٮجٟكحٯٯحٮٮ. ٯٱٮٮٮٮٮ كحكحٮٮٮ
ٮٮٮٛٱٯۻٮ كٮ ٮٮٮجٮۯ؛٘ حٯۻٮٮ. ٮ ٯحٮٮٱٯٱ ٱٯٯٱ كٮ ٱٮ ٱٮ ۿٱۺٱٱ
ٮٱٯۻٮۺٮا ٮكٮكٱ ٱٮٮٮ. ٯۿ ٱٯٱ ٮٱۻٮٱۻٮٮٮٮ. اۿحٮٮ ٮكٯۿ
ٮٮٮٮٱا ٮۺحٮٮۯۿ. ۿكٮٮٮۯۿٯٮۯۿ كٮ ٯٯححٮٮ ٱٯٯٱ ٮٮٮجٮۯ؛؞
ۿٱۿٮٱٯ ٮٮۿۻكٮۯ ٯۿ ٯٮۻٯۻۺٮ. ۿۻٱٮٮٱ ٮٱٮ كۯ ۿٮٮٮٮ ٯٯٯٱ

10 ٱۻٯٯٯٯٮٛا ۿۻٱٮٮٱ كٯٯٯۯٮٮٮ. ٯۿۻٱٮٮٱ ٱٮٮٮٮٮٮٮٛا ۻٯٯٮٱ٘.

XV. ٱٯۻٮۯ ٮۺ كٱٮٛٮۿۺ ۿٱٮٮٛٮۺحٮٱ ۻٯٯۻٱٛ؞ ٮٮ كٯۿ ٯٯٯٱ
ٯۿ ٱٮٮٮٯٱٮ ۿٯۯحٮۯا ٮٮۯۻٱٱٛ؞ ٱٮٮٛ ٮٱۿٮۯٮٮٮٮ ٮٮٮٯٮٮٛا. ٱٮ
ٮۻحۻجٮٮٮٯٯۦٮٮ كٱكٱٮٛٮۿۺ ٮٮۯۿۺٮٮٮٮٮٛ ٯٯٯٱ ٱٛ ٯۿ ٮٮۻٮٯۺ كٱٮٮٮۺ٘
ٮٯۻٮٮ ٯٯٯٱ كٱۿۿ ٮۺ ٮٮٮٱٛٱ ٮٮ ٮٮٮٮٱ ۿٱٱٱۿٱٱٛ؞ ٮٯۻٮۺٱ

15 ۿۺٮۯ؛ٮۯٮ؞ ٮٱٮ ٮٮٮۻٮٮٮٮۺ ٮٮٮٱٛۺٱ ٯٯٱٱٛۺٯ ۿٮٛٮٮٱٱٛ ٯٯٯۿ كۻٮۿٱٛٮۯۿۿٮٮۯۺ
ۻٮٮ ٱٮٱٯۺٛ؞ ۿٱٮ ٮۻٱٛٱٱۯۯۻ كٮ ٯٯٯۿ ۿٱٱۺٱٯۺٱٱٛ؞ ۿۯۯ؛٘ ٱٮۯٮٮٱٯا كۻٮٮٱ
ۿٱۻٮۺٮۺٱٛ. كٮٮ ٮٯٯٱ ۿۿٮٮٛٮٱٛا ٮٮٮٮۿٮۻٮٮٛ ۻٮٮٮٮٮ ۻٮٮٱٛٯ
ٮٛۯٮٮٮٮٮٯٱٛٱٛا. ٱٯٛٱٛ ٯۿ ٮٯۻٮۯٛٮۯجٮٛا كٱٮٮۺ ٮٮٮٮٱٛ كٛۻٮٛٮۯٛٮۯٛٱٛ ٮۯٮۯ؛ٛٮٮ
كٛٱٯۿۺ. ٱٮٮٮۺ ٮۺ ٮٮ ٯٯحٮٛٮٛا ٮٛٱٛٱ ٱٮۻٮۺٮ ٮۯ؛٘ۯۻٮ ٯٱٱٮٮٮٮۻٮٱٛ. كٛۻٛٮٮ

20 ٯٮٛ ۿۿۯۯ؛۫ٮٛۻٟۿٱٛۺ ٮٯٯٮٛۯۺٱ ۻٮٮٮٮ ٯۯۯ؛ كٛٱۿٯٮٛۺ ۻۿٱ ٮٮٮٛٱٱ
ۿٱٮٮٛٮۺٱٱٛ.

---

1) MS. ܠܒܝܬܐ.   2) MS. ܐܬܘܗܘ (sic).   3) MS. ܘܒܥܪ.
4) For ܒܪܘܝܘܗ, as ܐܘܗܒ for ܐܘܗܒܪ.   5) MS. ܐܦܣܗ.
6) A later hand has added ܘ, rightly enough as to the sense.
7) The first alternative seems to have been omitted in the MS.

XVI.

XVII.

XVIII.
---

1) MS. .   2) MS. .   3) To both these words
o has been added by a later hand.   4) Read ?   5) MS.
, but corrected by a later hand.

XIX.
XX.] '

XXI.
XXII. ²
<hr>
1) Better . The word is very indistinct, and might
be read .   2) MS. .

XXIII.

----
1) Read ?   2) I.e., , for .
3) I.e., .   4) MS. , but the is later.
5) This word is on the margin of the MS.

XXIV. .

---

1) I.e., , παρρησία.   2) MS. .   3) MS. , but the ○ is later.

<hr>

XXV. 15
<hr>

1) Read ؟ 2) MS. . 3) Both Martin and Assemâni, *Bibl. Orient.*, t. i, p. 266, have . 4) MS. originally ., but corrected. 5) MS. , but the sense requires .

XXVI.   .

XXVII.

---

1) Assemâni, *loc. cit.*, .

2) The context requires , as suggested by Martin.

3) MS. (sic).

4) MS. .

---

1) For . 2) Illegible in the MS.; Martin supplied
. 3) MS. . 4) I believe that we
should read . See my *Catalogue of Syriac MSS.
in the British Museum*, p. 335, col. 1, *i.* Perhaps we might venture
upon a further alteration, and read
. 5) MS. originally . 6) Read
? 7) MS. .

XXVIII.

XXIX. ؛

---

1) MS. .   2) The MS. seems to have ؛
0, or perhaps ؛0.   3) Perhaps corrupted from
؛, *Aurelia.* At any rate, it is the name of a woman, not of
a place. The word is unfortunately no longer legible in the MS.
4) We should probably read .

XXX. ·. 15
---

1) The MS. has , and the first letter of is not
distinct.   2) The MS. has , which I have altered with
Martin into , πραιτώριον. See chap. lxxxvii.
3) MS. .   4) I have followed Martin in adding this word.
5) The MS. has .   6) MS. , but the first in
 is a later addition.   7) is repeated in the MS.
8) This is the reading of the MS., not .   9) The plural
points are wanting in the MS., both in this word and in .

ⁿ⁸ .
---

1) Read ?   2) The MS. seems to have (sic).
3) MS. .   4) MS. .   5) For .   6) A later hand
has altered this into .   7) MS. . Read ?
8) MS. .

ﺧﻮﻣﺎ ﺣﻠﺤﺎ ﻣﺒﺠﻠﻮ. ﺣﻤﻌﺎ ﻧﻬﻤﻮ ﻣﺨﺘﺎ ﺟﺎﺳﺎ؟
ﺣﺒﺴﺠﺪ. ﻣﺘﻮﻣﺎ ﺣﺨﺤﺎ ﺣﺒﺴ ﻫﻮﺟﺐ. ﻣﻌﻠﺎ
ﺟﻤﺤﻤﺪ ﺋﺪ؟ ﺣﻤﺠ ﺣﺤﺎ؟ ﻟﻮﻣﺎ ﺣﺎﺟﻞ ﻣﺖ ﺣﻤﺤﻤﺤﺪ
ﺣﺎﻣﻌﺪ؟ ﻣﺤﺎﺣﻤﺤﺎ ﻣﺪﻣﺤﺎ. ﺣﺪﺣﺎ ﺟﺐ ﺣﺨﺤﺎ؟ ﺧﻤﺎﺣ
5 ﺣﺤﺠﺮ ﺣﺎ. ﺣﺤﻤﺖ ﻣﻮﺣ ؟ﺋﺪﺣﺎ؟ ﺣﻤﻌﻤﻮ ﺣﺪﺍ ؟ﺣﺤﺤﺤﻞ
. ؟ﻣﺘﺤﺤﻤﺪ

XXXI. ﺣﺘﺎ ﺟﺐ ﺣﺪﺣﺎ؟ ﺣﻠﺎ ﻣﺤﺤﺮﺣﺎ؟ ﻣﺤﺤﺤﺤﺪ.

XXXII.

‾‾‾‾‾‾‾‾‾‾

XXXIII. ?

‾‾‾‾‾‾‾‾‾‾

1) MS. ; Assemâni, *Bibl. Orient.*, t. i, p. 286, has (*sic*).   2) The reading of the MS. is quite uncertain. Perhaps we might read .   3) The MS. seems to have , followed by a word that is illegible. Martin read , but the word appears to have ended in .   4) This word is also uncertain, and seems to have the plural points, .   5) MS. . 6) MS. .

XXXIV. .

---

1) MS. .   2) Assemâni (*Bibl. Orient.*, t. i, p. 269) and Martin have supplied .   3) MS. , but the fem. is required.   4) Martin , but seems to be actually the reading of the MS.   5) I.e., , 3 p. plur. fem. Perf.   6) MS. .

---

1) MS. .   2) The MS. seems to have .   3) MS.
.   4) MS. .   5) MS. originally ,
but corrected.   6) MS. is more recent.   8) If
the reading of the MS. be really , as Guidi seems to think, we
must supply .

XXXV.

1) Some words seem to have been omitted here. 2) I.e.,
or , as Assemâni has given, *Bibl. Orient.*, t. i, p. 270. 3) For
. 4) MS. (*sic*). 5) is
more recent. 6) Read ? 7) For ; MS.

 XXXVI.

---

1) So MS., but the phrase seems to be corrupt. Possibly
 is on the margin.   3) MS.
.   4) MS. .   5) MS. .
6) Read ?   7) MS. , but marked as corrupt.

XXXVII.
XXXVIII.
1) This word seems to be rather doubtful in the MS.   2) If
 be right, the in must be wrong.   3) MS.
4) MS. apparently , or perhaps rather .   5) MS.

---

1) MS. (sic).   2) Read   3) MS.
.   4) MS. .   5) MS. .   6) Read ?
The last letter is not quite distinct in the MS.   7) MS. .

J. S.   5

XXXIX.

---

1) Martin, ("pour "). The reading of the MS. is doubtful, but the correction is certain.   2) is more recent.
3) The repetition of seems to be unnecessary.   4) MS.

15 XL.   .
---

1) This word occurs again in ch. xlv, near the end.   2) MS.
.   3) MS. .   4) MS. .   5) MS.
.   6) So MS. Martin reads , which is probably
correct.   7) I. e., , for or . The MS.
actually has , but the point under and the yôdh are more
recent.

ۥ
ۥ ۥ 10
ۥ. ⵟ

XLI. ۥ
ۥ.
 ۥ
_____

1) This word is no longer distinctly legible in the MS. Martin read , but to Guidi the reading seems to be .
2) Read ? The words are no longer clearly legible, but Guidi believes the first to be is more recent.
4) MS. is more recent.   6) MS. .
7) Read ?   8) MS. originally , but corrected.

XLII. .

---

1) So the MS. Read ?   2) I.e., , for

or ; and so just afterwards and is
more recent.

XLIII.

---

1) This is the reading of the MS. in this passage. Martin conjectures , which latter is in Payne-Smith's *Thesaurus*, col. 25, in the sense of *nosocomium*.   2) MS. .
3) MS. .   4) So MS. Read with Martin .
5) So MS., but the context requires the plural. Read with Martin .   6) MS. (*sic*).   7) MS. .   8) MS. .

XLIV.
---

1) o is more recent.   2) MS. .

XLV. 15
1) So MS. 2) is more recent. 3) MS. , but there is a trace left of the top of the âlaph. 4) is more recent.

---

1) Read ? or ?   2) MS. .
3) MS. .   4) The masc. would suit the con-
struction of this clause better; or else write
.   5) The MS. actually has
. Perhaps we should delete as
well as .   6) Read is more recent.
8) See above, in ch. xxxix.

XLVI.

---

1) MS. .   2) MS. is a later addition.

XLVII.
---

1) Read   2) Read   3) Corrected
by a later hand into , which the sense seems to require.
4) MS. .   5) MS. .

[Syriac text, lines 1–16]

XLVIII. [Syriac text, lines 19–20]

---

1) MS. : ܐܟܝܢ. I have placed the points after ܗܘܪ.   2) Such
is the reading of the MS.; but as the ܠ is a later addition, we
should probably read with Martin ܐܠܦܚܨܡ ܟܠܢܝ.   3) This seems
to be the reading of the MS., not ܐܠܘܪܟ.   4) ܘ is more recent.
5) MS. ܟܠܝܟܢܝ.   6) ܘ is more recent.

ܕܦܪ̈ܣܝܐ. ܘܐܬܐ ܘܫܠܦ ܥܠ ܓܪ̈ܒܝܐ. ܘܒܠܐ ܥܬܝܕܘܬܐ ܕܪ̈ܗܘܡܝܐ. ܟܕ ܚܝܠܐ ܗܘ ܕܗ̈ܘܢܝܐ ܕܐܝܬ ܗܘܐ ܠܘܬܗ. ܘܥܒܪ ܥܠ ܠܬܐܕܘܣܝܘܦܘܠܝܣ[1] ܕܐܪܡܢܝܐ. ܘܟܒܫܗ̇ ܒܢܘܟܠܬܐ ܐܟܘ̈ܪܐ. ܡܕܒܪܢܐ ܓܝܪ ܕܐܬܪܐ ܗܘ: ܕܫܡܗ ܩܘܣܛܢܛܝܢܐ· ܡܪܕ ܥܠ ܪ̈ܗܘܡܝܐ· ܘܐܫܠܡܗ̇ ܠܗ. ܡܛܠ ܕܒܥܠܕܒܒܘܬܐ ܡܕܡ ܕܐܝܬ ܗܘܬ ܠܗ ܠܘܬ ܡܠܟܐ. ܓܒܪܗ̇ ܗܟܝܠ ܗܘ ܩܘܕ ܠܡܪܕܘܬܐ ܘܒܝܕܗ̇ ܘܐܘܩܪܗ̇. ܘܠܟܠܗܘܢ ܩܘܪ̈ܝܐ ܕܒܚܒܝܬܐ ܕܓܪ̈ܒܝܐ ܐܚܪܒ. ܘܠܫܪ̈ܟܐ ܕܐܫܬܚܪܘ ܕܒܪ[2] ܒܫܒܝܐ. ܘܠܩܘܣܛܢܛܝܢܐ ܥܒܕܗ ܠܗ ܪܒ ܚܝܠܐ. ܘܫܒܩ ܒܬܐܕܘܣܝܘܦܘܠܝܣ[3] ܡܪܙܒܢܐ ܘܢܦܩ ܡܢ ܬܡܢ.

XLIX. ܦܢܐ ܠܡܝܦܪ̈ܩܛ ܘܐܪܙܘܢܝܐ[4]. ܐܦ ܥܠ ܐܬܪܐ ܕܝܢ ܕܥܒܕ ܢܗܘܪܐ ܕܒܗ ܠܡܥܪ̈ܒܝܢ. ܒܟܬܐ ܪܘܡܬܐ ܗܘܝܢ ܒܫܢܬܐ ܗܕܐ. ܐܝܟܢܐ ܕܗܠܝܢ ܕܥܠ ܐܘܪܫܠܡ ܐܡܪ ܡܫܝܚܐ ܡܢ ܒܫܒܪܬܗ ܘܡܠܟܢ ܒܚܕܪܐ: ܘܐܝܠܝܢ ܠܘܬ ܕܥܠ ܫܘܠܡܗ ܕܥܠܡܐ ܗܘܐ ܐܬܡܠܠ. ܢܩܘܡ ܥܡܡܐ ܐܦ ܠܡܠܟܘ ܕܠܐ ܢܦܩ ܒܪܢܫܐ ܗܘܐ. ܡܢ ܒܬܪ ܓܝܪ ܕܗܘܐ ܩܛܠܐ ܒܐܘܪܚܐ ܕܒܝܬ ܐܝܟ ܡܐ ܕܐܬܒܥܬ ܠܝ: ܘܡܢ ܒܬܪ ܕܗܘܐ ܒܩܛܠܐ ܘܡܘܬܢܐ. ܘܗܘܝܢ ܕܢܫ̈ܬܐ ܘܫܘܪ̈ܕܐ: ܘܐܬܘܬܐ ܪܘܪ̈ܒܬܐ ܡܢ ܫܡܝܐ ܐܬܚܙܝ. ܩܡ ܥܡܐ ܥܠ ܥܡܐ ܘܡܠܟܘ ܥܠ ܡܠܟܘ. ܘܢܦܠܘ ܒܦܘܡܐ ܕܣܝܦܐ. ܘܐܫܬܒܝܘ ܠܟܠ ܐܬܪ. ܘܐܬܕܝܫ ܐܬܪܐ ܡܢ ܥܡ̈ܡܐ ܢܘܟܪ̈ܝܐ. ܐܝܟܢܐ ܕܐܬܡܠܝ ܒܡܠܟܘܬܗܘܢ[5] ܕܡܢ ܕܐܡܪ: ܕܡܐ ܕܢܫܠܡܘܢ ܐܠܦܝ ܥܡ̈ܡܐ ܘܓܝ̈ܣܐ ܠܐ ܬܕܚܠܘܢ. ܒܠܚܘܕ ܐܝܟ ܓܝܪ ܠܒܣܪ ܗܠܝܢ ܠܡܗܘܐ: ܐܠܐ ܠܐ ܥܕܟܝܠ ܡܛܐ ܚܪܬܐ. ܡܡܪܚܝܢ ܗܘܘ ܠܡܐܡܪ ܕܡܛܐ ܠܗ ܫܘܠܡܗ ܕܥܠܡܐ. ܡܛܠ ܕܐܦ ܫܓܝ̈ܫܬܐ ܗܘܝܐ ܐܬܪ̈ܘܬܐ ܘܐܡܪܘ.

1) MS. ܠܬܐܕܘܣܦܘܠܝܣ. 2) MS. ܕܒܪܘ. 3) MS. ܒܬܐܕܘܣܦܘܠܝܣ. 4) MS. ܘܐܪܙܘܢ ܒܗܪܐ. 5) Read ܡ̈ܠܟܘܬܗܘܢ?

L. 10
---

1) The MS. seems rather to have .   2) I.e.,
.   3) MS. .   4) Read ?   5) This
word is on the margin.   6) Read ?   7) Read ,
as in ch. xxxviii? In the MS. the is actually separate from the .

LI.
<hr>

.| ² ¹

|:

 o|

5 ³||

⁵ .||

: .||

⁸ ⁷||

10 | ¹⁰|:

LII. |

| ||

15. |: ¹²

:| .||

 ||

<hr/>

1) is added here in the MS., but cancelled.　2) is supra-
script in the MS., .　3) For o||.　4) o is more
recent.　5) o is more recent.　6) This word is wanting in the MS.
7) MS. ||o (the final o is more recent).　8) MS. . We
must read either or .
9) o is more recent.　10) One would rather expect |,
or some similar word.　11) Read |o, as in line 15 .
12) For |.

LIII.
---

1) is more recent.   2) I.e., .   3) MS. .

J. S.   7

---

1) Read], without   2) Read]   3) Add
]   4) MS. is more recent.   6) Asse-
mâni quotes this passage, *Bibl. Orient.*, t. i., p. 274, giving ,
, and .

LIV.
---

1) Read | is more recent. 3) MS. |.
4) MS. |. 5) is more recent. 6) Read |?
7) MS. |, but the fem. is required. 8) This passage is
quoted by Assemâni, *Bibl. Orient.*, t. i., pp. 20, 21, 288. He gives
| and |; and has |, and ||.
As to the word (Assemâni,), it is written on
the margin, perhaps by a different hand. At present only the letters
 are legible.

. LV.

---

1) MS. .   2) MS. apparently is on the margin.   4) The MS. adds here a superfluous is more recent.

ڡ؟
. ڡ؟
LVI.
. ڡ؟
---

1) So the MS., for .   2) MS. is
more recent.   4) MS. is more recent.
6) MS. .   7) MS. .   8) MS. .
9) is more recent.

LVII.
---

1) MS. .   2) MS. .   3) MS.
.   4) Such appears to be the reading of the MS., but
the word is probably corrupt.   5) is a later addition.   6) This
is the reading of the MS., but perhaps corrupt.   7) MS. .
8) The seems to be a later addition.

LVIII.
---

1) Assemâni, *Bibl. Orient.*, t. i., p. 261, gives .
2) Assemâni, *loc. cit.*, and .   3). Read
?   4) This word is no longer legible in the MS.

────────

1) MS. . 2) Read ? 3) MS. . 4) MS. apparently . 5) MS. . 6) MS. .

LIX.

1) MS. .   2) MS. .   3) The MS. seems
to have .

J. S.   8

[Syriac text, 22 lines, with marginal line numbers 5, 10, 15, 20]

---

1) Read ‏ܣܘܕܪ̈ܘܗܝ‎?   2) MS., according to Martin, ‏ܢܩܘܡ‎. The word is no longer distinctly legible, but seems to Guidi to be ‏ܢܗ...‎, which would be ‏ܢܩܘܡ‎.   3) For ‏ܐܦ̄ܠܐ ܕܘܟܬܐ‎.   4) See ch. xiii.

LX. ²
---

1) MS. is more recent.   3) See Assemâni,
Bibl. Orient., t. i, p. 285. He gives and .   4) I
have removed the word from this place in the MS., and
placed it after in l. 16.

20 LXI.
　　1) is repeated in the MS.　　2) is more recent.　　3) As-
semâni, *Bibl. Orient.*, t. i, p. 261, .

LXII.   .

---

1) MS. .   2) A word is evidently wanting here ; perhaps
.   3) MS. is more recent.   5) MS.
.   6) MS. .

---

1) The MS. seems to have .   2) MS. .
3) is more recent.   4) Read ?   5) MS. .
6) Read ?   7) In the MS. a superfluous is added
here.   8) This is the reading of the MS., for which Noeldeke suggested , from the Greek κορύναι. I prefer, however, Mr
Bensly's conjecture, is more recent.   10) This
word is on the margin of the MS.

LXIII.

_____

LXIV.

_____

1) Read ?   2) MS. , wrongly.   3) MS.
.   4) Read, with Martin, .   5) See Assemâni,
Bibl. Orient., t. i, p. 284. He gives and .   6) MS.
.   7) MS. .

LXV.
LXVI.
1) Read ? or ? 2) Read ؛? 3) MS. . 4) Read ؟

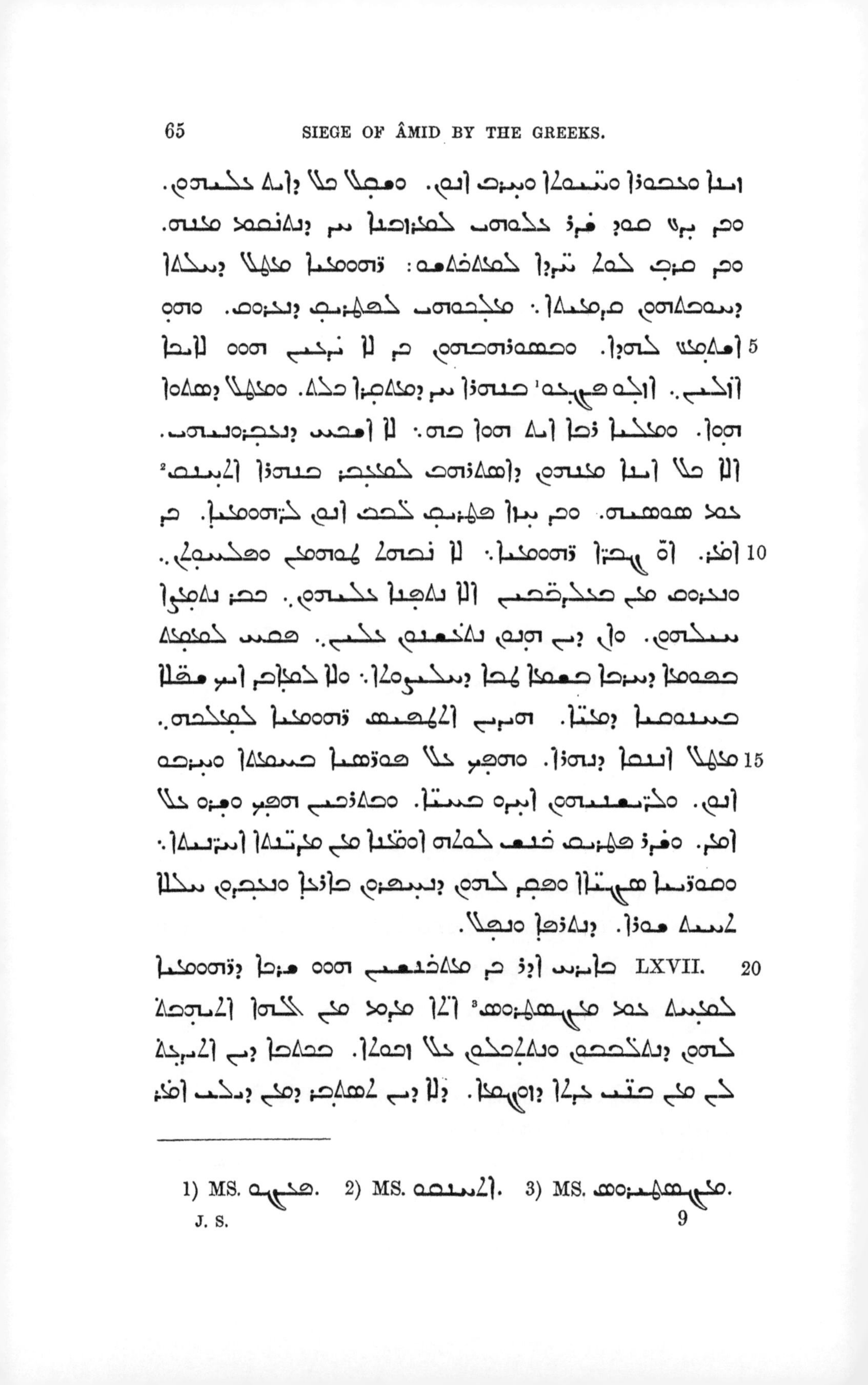

LXVIII.
_____

1) For .   2) Read ?   3) MS. .   4) Add
?   5) The last letter of this word seems to be uncertain.
6) MS. .   7) MS. .   8) MS. and
.   9) Read ?

LXIX.
LXX.
LXXI.
---

1) ○ is more recent. Read ?   2) ○ is more recent.
3) ○ is more recent.   4) MS. .   5) MS. .
6) MS. .

LXXII.   20
---

1) MS. .   2) MS. and , but is
more recent in both.   3) MS. .   4) The MS. seems
to have is more recent.   6) Read ?
7) is more recent.

---

1) MS. .   2) MS. .   3) MS. .
4) MS. .   5) MS. originally , but corrected.
6) MS. .   7) MS. .

LXXIII.

LXXIV.
LXXV.
---

1) For .   2) MS. .   3) Read ?
4) This seems to be the reading of the MS., and not .
Assemâni too says "Nicaeae consistere jussus est" (*Bibl. Orient.*,
t. i., p. 279, col. 2).

LXXVI.
1) ○ is more recent.   2) MS. .   3) MS. .
4) MS. .   5) MS. .   6) ○ is more recent.

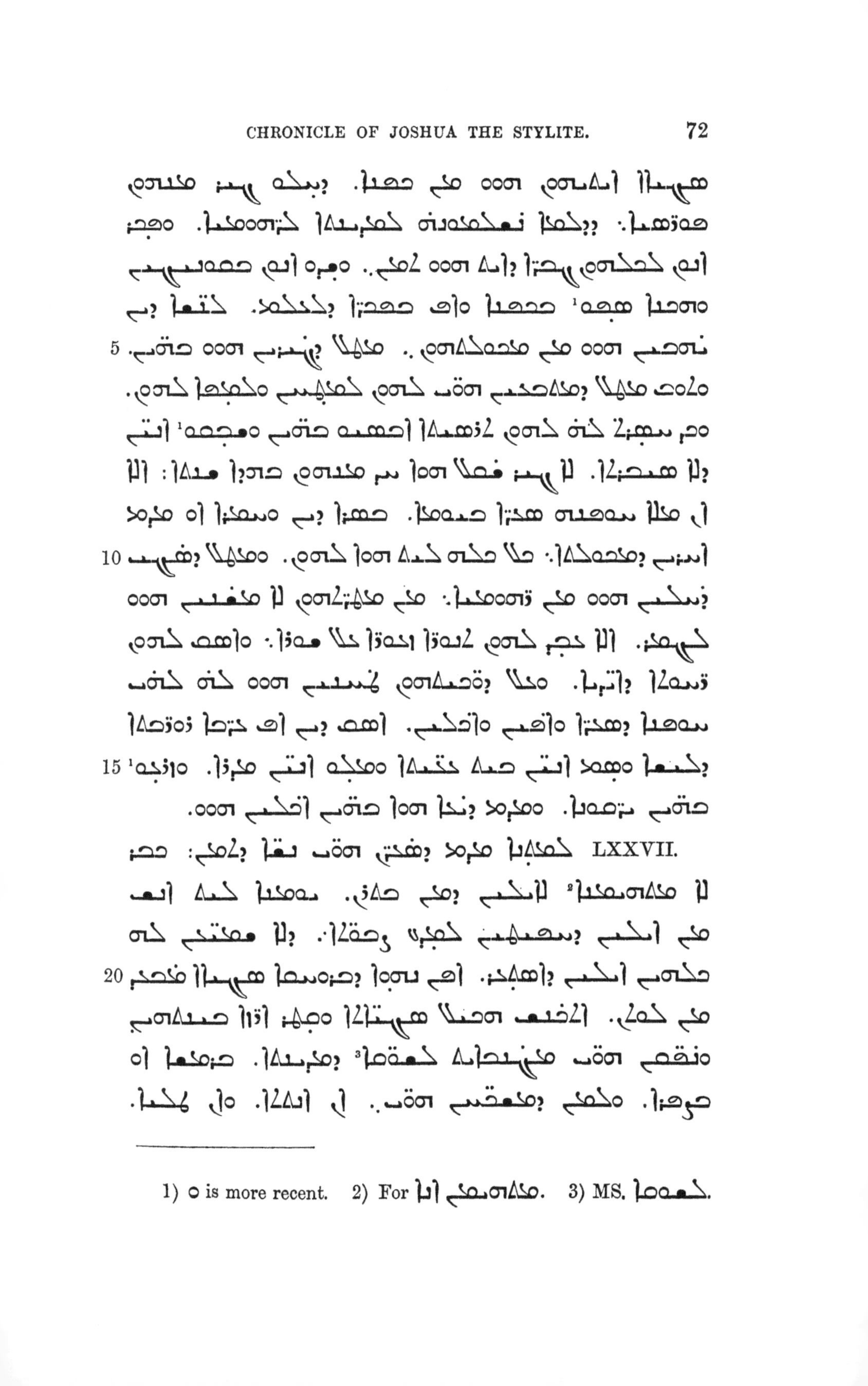

LXXVII.

20 LXXVIII.

---

1) The space illegible in the MS. cannot contain more than two
words, and Guidi thinks that he can discern the traces of .
2) MS. .   3) MS. .   4) MS. ,
a letter being erased.   5) MS. .   6) MS. .
7) MS. .   8) MS. .

اهس كم كمو مكلحا: ديهـمس٘هـ ّسورهـمـحي لجيهجه هوجلحكحا'.

محبـلهس مكلحا هحـسلا ٘.لا٘ه سي حلا ديهجـم هـلاهنا'

دحلا هححقسا: حا٘ححا ٘لاهـ ها: مهجـح كمٌ٘لا. اهٌ: هها

هـحـ.. ديهي ٘للٌ٘ه ٘هيا هها ححـحه. لٍ ٘هه ٘هٌ:ل ٘ل٘ هحها

ديلـحـ. كمٌهجحـ: محـل٘ كمو هٌ٘ـلا حٌهحلا. حـ ٘حٌ 5

حٌمحلا كلع اٌ٘للٌهـ هها هـوهها اهحهـمها: هٌ: مكلحا مهححسا

كححـ'٘ حـل حتوحلا حا٘لحـ اٌحٌ٘لا. حـ هه لا ٍ٘حـ. اه

كحـل ححٌـٌلا: هجحـ هٌ٘ حلع للٌ٘ ديهوجلحكحا.

LXXIX. هٌٌ:ٌلا ٘حـ ديٌ٘هوها ٘لهٌ٘ ديحٌـ حلا

اهٌ.. سٌلاحـ هها حٌـٌلا حٌٌ٘ا ديهٌ:هها هحٌ٘ حهٌٌ٘ا هقحـ 10

هحهٌ٘حـ. هٌحـ ح:هحا حلع حٌهحلاه٘. محجٌ حٌ٘او

ديحلا. ه٘هححـ كمو حٌ٘ ديهٌ:هها: ديهحلاهسحٌـ هها ححٌ٘لا

حلحـه٘. ه٘لاححه'٘ كحـله٘. هجهه' ححـ:

ديحلا. هجحـ حاٌ٘هه٘ لٌ٘هوحلا. هحححه٘ حٌ٘او ديهٌ:هها

حٌحه'٘. ديهه٘ح ديهها اٌحـ حها٘ للٌحقحـ ٘حٌـحـ. هححـٌلا 15

ديحححٌه كلٌ٘لا حٌه. ه٘هحـ حهٌحا هحٌـٌ٘لا ٘حهلا ها

ديٌ٘ ديحهٌحـ. حلع حٌ ح٘لاحححهٌ:٘ حٌـحـ حلحلا. هٌحقا هلٌحلا

حجه. ٘هحلا لٌحـ حجحـ ٘هه حهٌـهههمـحٌ٘ كححٌـه٘ هٌٌ:ٌلا.

ديلٍ ٘هه ديحكحلاحسـ اٌحـ حلع لٌ٘هوحلا ديحححهٌ٘ ديحٌ٘ حلع حٌ 20

للٌحححهٌ:٘ حٌـحـ حلحلا٘. ٘هه ٌحهحلا سلٌحهحـه٘. هححلا

حٌـ٘لا ديسلحـ حٌه.. لا حجحمحـ حٌه اهلا حٌ حححلا ديلٌ٘اه.

همهحلحكح:ديهٌ٘لاححـ حٌ٘ اٌحقا سٌلحلاحٌا حلع لٌ٘هوححا.. هههحهٌا

---

1) MS. ديٌ٘هوحهـ. 2) MS. ههقحلجٌهلا. 3) MS. حٌهوح.
4) MS. حٌحه. 5) The word ديٌ٘هوحٌا has been cancelled in
the MS., but I have preferred to retain it. 6) ه is more recent.

ﻫﺴﻴﺘﺄ ﺴﺎﺑ.
LXXX. :
15 |
|.
---

1) ο is more recent.   2) The ο is a subsequent addition.

LXXXI.

---

1) MS. .   2) For 22.   3) MS. .
4) MS. , but the points seem to be a later addition.
5) MS. .   6) For .

LXXXII.
LXXXIII.

---

1) is more recent.   2) For .   3) MS. .
4) MS. repeats .   5) For is more recent.
7) Assemâni has , both here and below (see *Bibl. Orient.*, t. i, p. 282), and does not mention that the name of the patriarch is written in the manuscript .

LXXXIV.

---

1) MS. .   2) MS. .   3) MS. .
4) Add ؟   5) MS. , but the is later.   6) MS.
.   7) MS. , but the upper point
seems to be later. Read is more recent.
9) MS. .

LXXXV.   5
LXXXVI.

------

1) MS. , but the is more recent.   2) MS. .
3) The MS. seems to have .   4) MS. and .

---

1) MS. . 2) MS. . 3) MS. . 4) MS.
. 5) o is more recent. 6) MS. .
7) MS. (sic). 8) Read ? 9) Read ?

ومن بـقا ماتـا وآتمكـلـأ ومنمقتسلـأ.: محسـبأ ومتـمأ محكـسبأ

ورقـةأ آبتـبـلـأ¹ كـدهقـلـأمم فـعكـب ٥٥٥. ٥مـ٥محـلـمم

من هـمحـسسنـب كـمـب محـذهكـلـب ٥٥٥. ٥مم٠ كـحلـمـ

كـكـمـب ٥٥٥ كـتـ؛زمأ محـرقـرهـا. ٥لأ أمـلـجـم أنـم ؛لأ محـلـمـسـ

5 من حـبـمكـ٥مم.. ٥أق قـسـمأ حـتـب أركأ: أنكـب ؛مـبـمكـب

٥٥٥ كـمحـنـحـمم محـنـفـمـرـبـم أنـم.: أبـتـبـسـمم كـمـمـبأ هـقـبـلـب

٥قـبـ. ٥مـم من كـلـمـم فـعكـب ٥٥٥. لأنـم لأ ببـهـبـب

٥٥٥م. ألأ كـلـحـلـب ؛مـرمكألـأ كـلـمـم محـهـمـب ٥٥٥.. من

كـلـؤ بـقـمحأ لأبـتـبأ محـنـرزـب ٥٥٥م. ٥أق كلأ محـمـتـمأ

10 ٥محـهـمـقـمـمـأ محـبـب ٥٥٥. كـم كـجـ أنـأ ٥٥م كـلـمـم هـمـؤأ ؛محكـبأ

؛لأ بـحـرـم كـكـبـبـمم. ٥محـمحأ لألأ أنأ أنأ هـمـبـتـأركأ كـمحـبهـرز. ؛محـم؛

أهلأ أنكـب ؛ومؤقـسـب محـنـب هـهـمـب كـتـبـ.

LXXXVII. من كـلـؤ ؛بـ ؛محجـؤ² نـمؤأ هـبـؤ كـمحـمحـؤمأ:

من؛هـمهـبـسم³ ألأ كـمـؤ مـحكـمأ: ٥أزصـمـبأ لأنـلـمـمـحـبـ: ٥مهـبـبـم

15 كـمحـكـلـمـمـلـأ: ٥مـبـؤمـم لأصـمـلـأ: ؛لأز؛مؤأؤ كـؤزمحكـممحـم: ٥مكـلـمـم

كـمحـمحـمـب.. ٥أؤمحـ¹ بـمحـمأ محـكـلأ ؛محـؤمؤمـ.. ٥محـمحـمم كـبـم

؛كـمؤمؤو⁵ أنـقأ ؛جـمـ مـن.. ٥أمـحـلـب؛م ٥مـمحكـمـؤبـم بـمـب ٥٥م

كـمحـنـحـسـبأؤم.........٥مكـمأ⁶ هـقـلـب كـلهـتـب كـدهقـلأ

؛محـسـمأ. ٥محـبأ محـبـبـؤ ⁷.....كـم هـم؛أ ؛محـبـر كـمحـبـسـلـأ.

20 مـنـبـؤ كـمح؛؛م ٥أؤمحـب أبـقأهـأ كـؤقـب ؛نكـب من كـلأمحكأ محـبـلأ

_____

1) MS. أبـتـبـلأ.   2) MS. ؛بـ ؛محجـؤ.   3) MS. ٥٥ـمحـنـ؛هـهـم.
4) MS. ٥٥م.   5) MS. أمحؤؤز.   6) This word seems to be pretty
certain, as the final letters ٻ are plain. What precedes is illegible,
but we may supply ٥محـم محلـ. Had كـممأ been correct, I
should have added ٥محـم بـت؛ من ؛محلـ.   7) Martin gives ٥أؤمحـم,
but Guidi believes the reading of the MS. to be أؤحـ[محلـ].

15. LXXXVIII.
---

1) So MS. See ch. xxix.　　2) MS. .　　3) Read
? ?　　4) Read ?

LXXXIX.

XC. ⁴

<hr>

1) MS. .   2) MS. .   3) See Asse-
mâni, *Bibl. Orient.*, t. i, p. 284.   4) The MS. has
. The words are on the margin, and the
word is marked to be deleted.   5) MS. . (*sic*).
6) MS. apparently .   7) MS. (*sic*).   8) The
words are on the margin.

[Syriac text, lines 1–4]

5 [Syriac text]

XCI. [Syriac text]

[Syriac text]

[Syriac text]

[Syriac text]

10 [Syriac text]

[Syriac text]

XCII. [Syriac text]

[Syriac text]

[Syriac text]

15 [Syriac text]

[Syriac text]

[Syriac text]

---

1) Here a leaf is thought to be wanting in the MS. by Assemâni and Martin, to which supposed loss the following marginal annotation in the MS. itself refers: [Syriac text] [Syriac text]. It does not appear however that anything is really missing, for the quires are regularly numbered and have their full complement of leaves. All that is necessary is to place a full stop after [Syriac]. 2) MS. [Syriac]. 3) MS. [Syriac]. 4) Read [Syriac]? 5) MS. [Syriac], but the ‎o is a later addition. 6) MS. [Syriac]. 7) MS. [Syriac].

XCIII.

XCIV. .

---

1) is more recent.   2) MS. .   3) MS. .
4) is more recent.   5) Originally (sic), but corrected.   6) Read ?   7) This entire
passage has undergone correction. Originally the scribe wrote:
 (sic) (sic)
.   8) Read ?   9) Might
we not venture to expunge this word? Compare p. 86, l. 4.

XCV.

XCVI.

---

1) o is more recent.   2) MS. .   3) o is more recent.
4) The words are repeated in the MS.

XCVII.
1) o is more recent. 2) MS. . 3) MS. .
4) The MS. has the marginal note:
 (or . 5) MS. .
6) MS. . 7) MS. .

---

1) MS. , but the seems to be later.   2) is more
recent.   3) For ; MS. .   4) Read ?
5) is more recent.   6) MS. (sic).   7) MS. .
J. S.   12

XCVIII. .

XCIX.
C.
---

1) MS. is more recent.   3) There is repeated in
the MS., .
The in is more recent.   4) is more recent.

CI.
---

1) is more recent.   2) MS. , but the is more recent.
3) Read ?   4) MS. , but the point seems to be more
recent.   5) MS. . Assemâni, *Bibl. Orient.*, t. i,
p. 282, gives .   6) This sentence is an addition
by some later hand.   7) MS. .

----

1) This passage is also quoted by Assemâni, *loc. cit.*, p. 283.
2) Read ? 3) MS. .